Mr Quigley's Revenge

A Play

Simon Brett

A SAMUEL FRENCH ACTING EDITION

FOUNDED 1830

SAMUELFRENCH-LONDON.CO.UK
SAMUELFRENCH.COM

FOR AMATEUR PRODUCTION ENQUIRIES

UNITED KINGDOM AND WORLD EXCLUDING NORTH AMERICA

plays@SamuelFrench-London.co.uk

020 7255 4302/01

Each title is subject to availability from Samuel French,

depending upon country of performance.

MR QUIGLEY'S REVENGE

Commissioned by Kate Vaughan for the Chichester Festival Youth Theatre and first performed by them in the Minerva Theatre, Chichester, on 17th March 1994, with the following cast:

Bernard Millington	Johan Buckingham
Revd Jim Elkins	Daniel Fearn
Georgina Hewlett	Anna Scaife
Lydia Millington	Rosie Freshwater
Joan	Rosie Leaver
Keith Horrobin	Neil Morris
Mr Quigley	James Thorpe
Ivor Quigley	Alex Hartman
Lord Grevesham	Sebastian Finley
Tina	Katie Watts
Davina Horrobin	Georgina Downs
Candida Horrobin	Lucy Betts
Paula Hewlett	Gemma Thorogood
Patti	Vicky Andrews
Kelly	Beth Ockwell
Henrietta	Joanne Horstead
Tina's Class	Clementine Chamberlain
	Renata Champion
	Ros Cumberland
	Harriet Freshwater
	Kirstie Pritchard
	Stacey Williams
Rod	Tom Pook
Veronica	Tessera Perschke
Martyn Graves	Robin Lander Brinkley
Benji Sparrow	Jon Dedman
Ed Quigley	Nick Ashdown

Actors	Matthew Andrews
	Blaise Tapp
Tracey	Rebecca Hawkes
Dan	Mark Ashdown
Charlie	Michael Leasure
Youth Group	Helen Conford
	Clementine Chamberlain
	Renata Champion
	Harriet Freshwater
	Beth Jeavons
	Sandra Lee
	Matty Tristram
	Stacey Williams
	Matthew Andrews
	Simon Ashdown
Soldiers	Beth Jeavons
	Sandra Lee
	Matty Tristram
	Matthew Andrews
	Simon Ashdown
	Tom Betts
	Blaise Tapp
Jack	Richard Evans
Chloe	Colomba Giacomini
Jessica	Libby Freshwater
Antonia	Hannah Tristram
Beatrice	Catherine Williams
Araminta	Rebecca Carter
Perpetua	Emily Gordon
Professor Phun	Tom Godfrey
Kylie Quigley	Keshira Aarabi
Anneka Quigley	Eleanor Mason

Directed by Kate Vaughan
Designed by Adrian Whitaker

CHARACTERS
(in order of appearance)

Bernard Millington
Revd Jim Elkins
Georgina Hewlett
Lydia Millington
Joan
Keith Horrobin
Mr Quigley
Ivor Quigley
Lord Grevesham
Tina
Davina Horrobin
Candida Horrobin
Paula Hewlett
Patti
Kelly
Henrietta
Tina's Class—as many female extras as available
Rod
Veronica
Martyn Graves
Benji Sparrow
Ed Quigley
Amateur Actors—a few extras
Tracey
Dan
Charlie
Youth Group—as many (male and female) extras as available
Soldiers—as many (male and female) extras as available
Jack
Chloe

Jessica
Antonia
Beatrice
Araminta
Perpetua
Professor Phun
Kylie Quigley
Anneka Quigley

14 Male Speaking Parts
20 Female Speaking Parts

(This cast list can be cut down, or augmented with extras—the Chichester Youth Theatre production featured a cast of forty-six. For instance, the number of Candida's party guests can be adjusted according to availability of seven-year-old girls. Other passages can also be varied. For example, the Chichester production was fortunate to have a skilled unicyclist and juggler for the part of Professor Phun but the part and action would still work with a children's entertainer who stayed on his own two feet.)

SYNOPSIS OF SCENES

ACT I

Scene 1   Monday

Scene 2   Tuesday

Scene 3   Wednesday

Scene 4   Thursday

ACT II   Saturday week

The action of the play takes place in the Lesser Hall of the Frinsley Village Hall

Time—the present

ACT I

SCENE 1

The setting throughout is the Lesser Hall of the Frinsley Village Hall. The building dates from the late nineteenth century, and hasn't undergone major redecoration since the 1950s. The visible walls are painted up to about four foot in institutional pale green, and above that in what was once cream. Lights with wide metal shades hang over the space

The floor is covered with worn lino, stained by a thousand coffee spills— and worse. There are indistinct lines where it was once marked out for badminton or some other game. Fresh coloured tape marks out parts of the set for rehearsals of the Frinsley Amateur Dramatic Society's forth- coming production of Julius Caesar

There are six entrances to the Lesser Hall. DC *is the entrance from the car park. During the play, everyone coming in from outside uses this entrance. The* DL *and* UL *entrances lead to either side of the stage at the end of the adjacent Great Hall, which is used as a theatre by the amateur dramatic society*

The UR *entrance leads off to the toilets and changing rooms, as indicated by a pointing arrow. There are rows of hooks for coats by this entrance. At the back of the stage, right of* C, *is a door which leads to Mr Quigley's cubby-hole, a small room which the caretaker has made his own. To the left of this, fairly central, are double doors over which a grubby sign proclaims the room inside to be the "Sydney Pratt Memorial Room". In the wall between these doors and the* UL *entrance is a serving hatch (currently closed), which opens on to the Sydney Pratt Memorial Room*

Hanging high on the wall between the Sydney Pratt Memorial Room door and the hatch is a rather grubby lifebelt, encircling a shield bearing some indistinct armorial bearings, which presumably commemorates some

long-forgotten red-letter day in the history of Frinsley's sea cadets. An old-fashioned wall-mounted calendar reads "Monday 7th", the date on which the action of the play begins

It is evening, towards the end of a meeting of the Frinsley Village Hall Committee. A green baize-covered table surrounded by seven chairs is pre-set C to be seen by the audience as they come in. On the table are water carafes and glasses, as well as agendas, note-pads and pencils

When the House Lights go down, the six members of the committee take their seats during the Black-out. At the head of the table sits Bernard Millington, chairman of the village committee, a neat and fussy man in his late forties. He has a filofax which he keeps consulting, and his agenda is marked up with fluorescent highlights. Throughout the scene, he keeps sipping water from the glass in front of him

On his left sits Joan, secretary of the village committee. She is a mousy unmarried woman of indeterminate age, who speaks in a little voice and assiduously takes minutes in a shorthand notebook throughout the committee proceedings

Next to her sits the Revd Jim Elkins, the local vicar, one of the hearty kind who keeps saying he won't talk about religion, and then does

Next to the vicar sits Keith Horrobin, an attractive and plausible man in his thirties, who is very bright and knows it. He wears a smart suit and brightly-coloured tie. In front of him on the table is his portable phone. He takes acute interest in the proceedings of the committee, but somehow gives the impression that he is rather above it all

Opposite Keith sits Bernard's wife, Lydia Millington. She is in her early forties, fighting a rearguard action against the fading of her charms. The form this takes is a rather overt flirtatiousness towards anything in trousers—except of course her husband. Lydia is bored by the committee proceedings, and making very little attempt to hide the fact. She is, however, very interested in Keith Horrobin

Beside her, and on Bernard Millington's right, sits the final member of the committee, Georgina Hewlett, a bossy country lady who looks as though she should have a couple of Labradors with her

At the opposite end of the table from Bernard is an empty chair

Bernard's voice starts in the Black-out, and the Lights slowly fade up to indicate that the committee meeting has already been going on for some time

Bernard ...and it would therefore be my proposal, as Chairman, that we endeavour in future to minimise the number of subcommittees appointed by the Frinsley Village Hall Committee.

Revd Elkins But why, Mr Chairman?

Georgina (*rather short-temperedly*) Obviously, because it'll simplify our procedure, vicar.

Bernard (*clearing his throat*) Erm. Georgina, I must request that you address your remarks through the chair, please.

Georgina Oh, I do beg your pardon, Mr Chairman. (*Rather short-temperedly to Revd Elkins*) Mr Chairman, obviously because it'll simplify our procedure, vicar.

Bernard Now of course, though we can in future limit the number of subcommittees, we do have a short-term problem of how we deal with those subcommittees already set up. For instance, you, Reverend Elkins, have got your subcommittee on countering the menace of toilet roll thefts. Going well, is it?

Revd Elkins (*making his little joke*) Definitely on a roll.

Bernard (*ignoring the witticism*) And then Joan's heading the subcommittee on——

Lydia (*having had quite enough of this*) Oh, for heaven's sake, Bernard, get on with it! We all know what subcommittees have been set up.

Bernard (*with injured dignity*) Lydia, I must ask you to address your remarks through the chair.

Lydia I'm your wife, for God's sake, Bernard! I don't have to address you through the chair.

Bernard I'm afraid, for the purposes of this committee, we cease to be husband and wife and become simply Chairman and committee member. Now, next...

Joan So how do I minute that, Mr Chairman? The Chairman's wife then interrupted with...?

Bernard You *don't* minute that, Joan. (*He tries to reassert his control*) So, the problem is ... what do we do about the existing subcommittees?

Keith Might I suggest, Mr Chairman, that as of this moment we disband all existing subcommittees?

Bernard Good heavens. That's a rather bold step, Keith.

Keith If we really do want to simplify our procedure, that's the way to do it, Mr Chairman.

Bernard True, Keith. Good executive decision-making. I see you haven't been wasting your time in all those local council meetings.

Keith smiles complacently

However, I do feel that in this instance your proposal is a little extreme.

Keith shrugs an only-trying-to-help shrug. Lydia reaches her foot across under the table and rubs it along his leg

And I think a more fruitful short-term measure in dealing with the proliferation of subcommittees of the Frinsley Village Hall Committee will be to appoint a subcommittee to investigate the problem.

Georgina, Revd Elkins and Joan react enthusiastically to this idea

Right. So, all those in favour...?

Georgina, Revd Elkins and Joan raise their hands. Keith and Lydia exchange wry eye contact

Excellent. I declare the motion carried and ... since you three are in favour, may I suggest that you are the ones who form the subcommittee...?

Revd Elkins (*very enthusiastically*) Fine by me.

Georgina (*very enthusiastically*) Certainly.

Joan (*very enthusiastically*) Oh yes.

Bernard (*rubbing his hands with satisfaction*) Good, we are getting on at a rate of knots, aren't we? (*He consults his agenda*) Now, on to the twelfth item on our agenda—which I've personally highlighted in green—"Mr Quigley".

All committee members sigh and shake their heads knowingly

Lydia Do we want to bring him in yet?

Bernard glares at her. She concedes with bad grace

Mr Chairman.

Bernard No, not yet. Where is he, by the way?

Lydia (*indicating the relevant door*) Through there. In his little cubby-hole. Probably having a snooze.

Bernard Oh, really?

Lydia Yes, he's got a bed in there. And a television, everything. He's made it very cosy.

Bernard (*after shaking his head with disapproval*) Now, Keith, I believe you've done a little investigation into Mr Quigley...?

Keith Yes, Mr Chairman. (*He rises to his feet and takes control of the meeting*) The fact is that Mr Quigley has been caretaker of the Frinsley Village Hall for most of his working life ... a working life which, in the nature of things, is coming to an end. Now, Mr Quigley has discharged his duties admirably over the years, but times change and I'm not sure that his ... leisurely, laid-back approach is entirely appropriate for the lean and accountable nineties.

Bernard So what is your conclusion?

Keith My conclusion, Mr Chairman, is that Mr Quigley should be retired as soon as possible.

Bernard Mm.

Georgina I would just like to say—if I may, Mr Chairman——

Bernard nods acquiescence

—that the old boy does do a good job. I mean, with the number of different clubs and parties that use this hall ... and Mr Quigley does all the bookings for them. He enters them up in his little blue book and he never gets anything wrong.

Keith May I speak directly to Georgina, Mr Chairman?

Bernard Please do, Keith.

Keith (*addressing Georgina*) I'm not disagreeing with anything you say, Georgina. Mr Quigley has done Frinsley Village Hall sterling service, as I'm sure will be recognised in the speeches at his farewell party. But as the Village Hall itself changes, so the requirements for running it will inevitably be different.

Georgina How'd you mean—"as the Village Hall itself changes"?

Keith looks at Bernard, as if to say, "Can I answer this?" Bernard nods permission

Keith The fact is—as our Chairman and some other members of the committee will be aware—there are hopes that this Village Hall—which you only have to look around you to realise is in a serious state of disrepair—may soon be replaced by a more modern complex.

Revd Elkins But how would that be paid for? There's hardly anything in the Village Hall Fund.

Keith No, so the money might have to come from other sources.

Georgina What other sources?

Keith looks to Bernard to check whether he can say more

Bernard I don't think it would be appropriate to go into that at this moment, Georgina. The situation is currently rather delicate...

Lydia And no official planning application has yet been put forward.

Bernard (*after a little grimace of annoyance at not being addressed as chairman*) No. Precisely. As Lydia has pointed out—and she should know, being on the local Planning Committee—no official planning application has yet been made. (*To Joan*) Erm, I think, Joan, we should keep this part of our discussion off the record.

Joan From where, Mr Chairman?

Bernard From the beginning of our discussion about the possible new Village Hall.

Joan Oh, right. (*She scribbles out something in her notebook and sits back, bored*) Make sure you tell me when to start again.

Bernard (*after a look of slight annoyance at her*) Yes.

Georgina Mr Chairman, I think it would be relevant to point out that a lot of local people are very attached to this hall.

Bernard I'm aware of that, Georgina.

Georgina There's a conservation lobby in the Frinsley area—and I'm one of them—who would favour refurbishing the existing Village Hall rather than knocking it down to build something new.

Bernard We are all entitled to our opinions, Georgina, and at the appropriate time all those opinions will be taken into account.

Lydia A lot of people round here are fond of Mr Quigley, too. They won't want to see him booted out.

Bernard Perhaps not.

Keith Which, Mr Chairman, is all the more reason to "let him go" as quickly and quietly as possible. The last thing we need is a local folk hero as a focus for the conservation lobby.

Bernard Exactly. This will of course mean someone has to undertake the ... slight unpleasantness of telling Mr Quigley about his future.

Lydia Or lack of one.

Keith If no-one else wants to do it, it's a task I would be prepared to undertake myself, Mr Chairman.

Bernard That's very unselfish of you, Keith.

Keith shrugs modestly. Bernard continues a little apprehensively

Are you proposing that it should be done at this committee meeting?

Keith No, no. Better on a one-to-one basis. Friday would be the ideal timing. I find it's always best to sack people on a Friday.

Revd Elkins So that they can have the weekend to get over it?

Keith No. More so that I can enjoy *my* weekend. (*He gets out his personal organiser and consults it*) Ah no, can't do Friday this week. (*Pressing a few keys on the organiser*) I'll do it Thursday evening.

Revd Elkins Oh. But surely——

He is interrupted by the ringing of Keith's portable phone

Keith Mr Chairman, I know this is terribly bad manners, but I'm expecting a rather important business call. Would you forgive me if I...?

Bernard (*with a gracious inclination of his head*) Of course. Please go ahead, Keith.

Keith rises from the table and comes down stage, switching his call through

Keith Hallo? (*He is disappointed at who it is*) Look, I'm sorry, darling, I'm in the middle of a meeting. I'll call you later. Goodbye. (*He switches off the phone and comes back to the table*) Sorry, false alarm.

Lydia looks at him with something approaching suspicion

Davina.

Lydia nods acceptance

(*He explains to the rest of the committee*) My wife.

Bernard Ah. (*He looks at his watch*) Well, perhaps we ought to bring Mr Quigley in now.
Lydia (*rising from the table*) I'll get him.

She goes across to the door to Mr Quigley's cubby-hole. As she does so, Keith's portable phone rings again

Bernard Well, you are the popular one, aren't you?
Keith (*with a helpless gesture to Bernard*) May I, Mr Chairman...?
Bernard Go ahead.

Keith rises from the table and moves down stage again, switching his call through. During his speech, Lydia knocks again on Mr Quigley's door

The door is grudgingly opened and Mr Quigley stands there. He is an amiable old boy in his sixties, dressed in an old-fashioned brown overall. He is unafraid of anyone, and enjoys sending up Bernard and the rest of the committee. He carries a battered blue engagements diary, which contains the Village Hall bookings

Lydia says that the committee's ready for him, and he crosses without enthusiasm to sit in the vacant chair at the other end of the table from Bernard. By this time Keith's telephone conversation will have ended

Keith (*into the phone*) Hallo? (*Pleased and honoured by who's calling him*) Oh, *hallo*, my lord. Yes, well, if you could come and view the premises, that'd be... Tomorrow evening, fine. Six thirty, excellent. I'll look forward to seeing you then. Goodbye. (*He switches off the phone and moves back to take his seat*) That *was* the business call.
Bernard Good-evening, Mr Quigley. I hope we haven't kept you waiting.
Mr Quigley No trouble. I got to hang around to lock up, anyway.
Bernard Good.
Mr Quigley Mind you, make it snappy, 'cause I like to get down the *Queen's Head* for a couple of pints before they close.
Bernard Yes. Erm, Mr Quigley, this is a committee meeting——
Mr Quigley Well, I know that, 'cause I've booked it in my little blue book, haven't I?
Bernard ——and I would appreciate it if you could address your remarks through the chair.

Mr Quigley (*bewildered*) Eh? (*He rises to stand back and look at his chair*) Through the chair, did you say?
Bernard Yes. Erm, don't worry about it. Do sit down, Mr Quigley.

With a shrug, Mr Quigley sits down

Joan, could you please start taking minutes again now?

Long-suffering, Joan moves forward to her shorthand notebook

Now, Mr Quigley, today's committee meeting is one of the two in the year when we ask you to report on the running of the Village Hall. (*He consults his filofax*) I've marked the date with a yellow sticker. I always use a yellow sticker for you, Mr Quigley.
Mr Quigley Oh, honoured, I'm sure.
Bernard (*uncertain whether he's being sent up or not*) Excellent. So, Mr Quigley, fire away.
Mr Quigley Right you are. Well, this year we've done good business on the wedding receptions. Mind you, downturn of a lot of weddings is, you get confetti over everything. And rice. Tell you, had one wedding where they threw rice ... and it rained. Blimey, in the car park it was like wading through rice pudding.

Revd Elkins is amused by this. Bernard is not amused by it

Bernard Yes. Mr Quigley, if you could move along...
Mr Quigley Right. So, wedding bookings up—kids' birthday parties down. Not that it bothers me, mind—wouldn't bother you neither if you'd spent as much time as I have getting jelly out from behind the radiators.

Once again, the vicar is amused. Once again, Bernard is not amused

Bernard Mr Quigley, just the facts, please.
Mr Quigley Right you are. (*He gets up and wanders round the table as he details the bookings*) Regular evening bookings doing fine. That's Mondays usually free, except first one of every month when you have this committee... Tuesdays you got your aerobatics...
Georgina Aerobics.

Mr Quigley Like I said—aerobatics. Won't believe the way they do the aerobatics now, Mr Millington. These days they got these little steps they go up and down on. Blimey O'Reilly. Apparently pay money for 'em, an' all. Good marketing that, innit? Get people to forget they got stairs and pay fifty quid to have their own private one. Mind you, maybe some of the ones who do it live in bungalows; that's probably it. (*To Georgina*) You live in a bungalow, do you, lady?

Georgina (*affronted by the idea*) Certainly not.

Bernard If we could move along a bit, Mr Quigley...

Mr Quigley Yeah, sure. So... Wednesday evenings we have the amateur dramatic lot in, don't we? The FRAUDS...

Lydia The FADS. Frinsley Amateur Dramatic Society.

Mr Quigley Oh, that's right. You're one of them an' all, aren't you, Mrs Millington?

Lydia Yes.

Mr Quigley Play all the big parts, don't you?

Lydia (*modestly*) Well...

Mr Quigley What's the show you're working on at the moment, remind me?

Lydia *Julius Caesar.*

Mr Quigley Oh, and I bet you're playing Julia, aren't you?

Lydia No, I——

Mr Quigley You know, my boy Ivor, he helps out with the sound for the amateur dramatics. Since he lost his missus, well, time kind of hangs heavy on his hands and he needs to——

Bernard clears his throat pointedly

Right. Then Thursday it's your lot, padre...

Revd Elkins My Youth Club, yes.

Mr Quigley All swigging vodka and smoking and canoodling out in the car park.

Revd Elkins (*affronted*) I can assure you that I have never seen any of my Youth Club members doing any such thing.

Mr Quigley No, but that's because they do it when you're not watching.

Revd Elkins is about to argue, but doesn't get the time

My grandson Ed, he goes down the Youth Club. (*He winks at Georgina*) Got the hots for your daughter, you know, Mrs Hewlett.

Georgina (*very frostily*) Paula no longer goes to the Youth Club, Mr Quigley. She seemed to be mixing with some rather rough types down there, I'm afraid.

Revd Elkins Oh, come on, Georgina, it takes all sorts——

Bernard We are meant to be hearing from Mr Quigley, Jim.

Revd Elkins Yes, of course, Mr Chairman.

Mr Quigley So where are we...? Right. Fridays no regular bookings. Then Saturday evenings is the judo club. Ivor's little girls do that. My granddaughters... Kylie and Anneka. Lovely kids they are. You know the little tinkers got my——

Bernard Yes, thank you, Mr Quigley. And are you finding any problems with the hall that we ought to know about?

Mr Quigley Well, latest thing is the lights keep going funny.

Bernard In what way "going funny"?

All the Lights suddenly go out, creating total darkness

Mr Quigley Bit like that. Got a good sense of timing an' all, haven't they?

General confusion from committee members as they rise to their feet. Mr Quigley moves in the darkness to his cubby-hole

Don't you worry about it. I can get 'em back on for tonight. Get Ivor to have a look at 'em tomorrow.

Lydia (*in a sultry whisper*) Are you going to be able to stay for a bit after the meeting?

Revd Elkins (*amazed*) I beg your pardon?

Mr Quigley opens the door of his cubby-hole. Light spills out to reveal that Lydia is facing the Revd Elkins. She moves away in confusion towards Keith

Mr Quigley closes the door

Joan I'm not taking minutes of anything that's said while the lights are off. Is that all right, Mr Chairman?

Bernard (*testily*) Yes, Joan, of course it's all right.

The Lights suddenly come back on. Keith and Lydia, who have been very close together, spring apart. Bernard does not notice this

Mr Quigley comes back beaming from his cubby-hole

Mr Quigley There. What would you do without me, eh?

Bernard and Keith exchange looks. Bernard clears his throat. The committee members move back to their seats. Mr Quigley comes forward to take up his seat

Now where were we?

Bernard I don't think we need bother you any more, Mr Quigley. You've given us all the information we need. Thank you very much.

Mr Quigley Oh, right. (*He looks at his watch*) Going to be much longer then, are you?

Bernard No, no. Just date of our next meeting and Any Other Business.

Mr Quigley Right you are then. I'll just tidy up.

He goes through into his cubby-hole

Bernard So… Item Thirteen on the Agenda. Diaries out for date of next meeting.

Georgina Well, it'll be the first Monday again, won't it? It always is. So that's the fourth.

Bernard (*checking in his filofax*) Yes. Precisely. And there it is. I always put a red sticker for Village Hall Committee meetings.

Georgina Except when Mr Quigley comes. Then you said you put a yellow one.

Bernard No, I put a red one *and* a yellow one. You see, the red one says "committee meeting", and then if there's anything special about the committee meeting, I've got a rather clever colour-coded system for——

Joan (*clearing her throat pointedly*) So is the meeting over?

Bernard What? Oh, right. No. First, Item Fourteen on the Agenda— which in fact I've highlighted in purple—Any Other Business. So … round the table. Any other business, Joan?

He looks at each of the committee members in turn and each responds. The responses are very quick

Joan No.

Revd Elkins No.
Georgina No.
Lydia No.
Keith No.
Bernard Good. (*He looks at his watch*) So the Chairman declared the
meeting ended at … nine forty-three p.m. Thank you very much, ladies
and gentlemen.

*All the committee members rise quickly. Joan, Georgina, and the Revd
Elkins go straight to the* UR *entrance, where their coats are hanging. Keith,
Lydia and Bernard linger*

Lydia Are you going for a drink, Bernard?
Bernard You know better than that, dear. (*He opens his filofax*) Going
for a drink's Friday. Look—green sticker.
Lydia Well, I'll see you at home then.
Bernard But——
Lydia I came directly from work. We're in two cars, remember?
Bernard (*going across to get his coat*) Oh, of course we are.

*As soon as Bernard's back is turned, Lydia looks significantly at Keith,
who grins back. Joan, Georgina, and the Revd Elkins have got their
coats and cross, one by one, to the* DC *exit. Keith and Lydia, still looking
at each other, give small acknowledgements of their goodbyes*

Joan Good-night.
Georgina Goodbye.
Revd Elkins See you soon.
Bernard (*coming back across the stage with his coat on*) Bye. (*To Lydia
and Keith*) You on your way?
Keith Minor planning question I need to ask Lydia. Just a quickie.
Bernard Right. (*He crosses to the* DC *entrance*) Goodbye, Keith.
Keith Goodbye.
Bernard See you later, dear.
Lydia Yes, dear.

Bernard goes out

Lydia and Keith stand facing each other in silence for a moment

You've got a nerve. (*She giggles*) "Just a quickie."

She suddenly moves across to him and they go into an ardent embrace. After a moment, Keith draws back a little: interested, but also quite relieved things can't go any further at that point

Keith Pity we haven't got anywhere we can go.
Lydia (*drawing out of the clinch and winking*) Leave it with me.

Keith watches with interest, as Lydia goes across to knock on the door of Mr Quigley's cubby-hole

Mr Quigley opens it

If you don't want to miss your drink, Mr Quigley, give me the keys and I'll lock up for you.
Mr Quigley Oh, that's very kind of you, Mrs Millington. Just get my coat.

Mr Quigley disappears back inside the cubby-hole

He evidently switches off some lights, because the stage lighting diminishes. Lydia looks back in triumph to Keith

Keith Very smooth indeed.
Lydia Thank you, kind sir.
Keith Almost as if you'd done it before.
Lydia (*lightly*) Don't be ridiculous.

Mr Quigley comes out of the cubby-hole, which he locks behind him. He is wearing his coat. He hands the keys to Lydia

I'll bring them to you in the snug before closing time.
Mr Quigley Bless you, Mrs Millington. (*He moves to the DC exit*) See you shortly, then.

Mr Quigley exits

Lydia (*calling after him*) Right you are. (*She dangles the keys from her fingers, moves across to the cubby-hole, and unlocks it. She looks sexily back at Keith*) Now about this planning query of yours...

Keith (*sexily, with heavy innuendo*) Yes, well, I've done my survey and made my application, you see, Mrs Millington ... and I'm just wondering when I'm likely to get permission to ... lay the foundations.

Lydia Oh, I don't think you'll encounter any delay about that, Mr Horrobin.

She moves sexily through into the cubby-hole. Keith hurries in after her. They are heard to giggle

The door closes behind them as the Lights snap to Black-out

SCENE 2

During the Black-out, the committee tables and chairs are struck, and the calendar changed to "Tuesday 8th"

Mr Quigley is standing DC, looking up at the hanging lights. He is illuminated in a flash of light

Mr Quigley (*calling out to someone unseen*) Yes, they're working.

The Lights immediately go out again

No, they're not.

The Lights come on again

Yes, they are.

The Lights go off again

No, they're not.

All the Lights come on except for the DC one Mr Quigley is standing directly beneath

Some of them are.

Ivor enters from Mr Quigley's cubby-hole. He is a good-natured—

though not very bright—working man in his early forties. He wears a tool-belt, full of screwdrivers, hammers, etc.

Ivor (*seeing the light that's not working*) Still that one.
Mr Quigley Yes, Ivor. Still that one.
Ivor (*shaking his head*) Have to go up there to fix it. (*He moves down stage*) Whole system needs rewiring, really.

Their conversation continues while Ivor goes to get a ladder, which he sets up underneath the faulty light. Preoccupied with the work in hand, he only half-listens to his father

Mr Quigley Everything in the hall needs work. They got some money in that Village Hall Fund, you know, but they keep putting off the decision to spend it.
Ivor Yeah. Well...
Mr Quigley Maybe you'll have better luck than me persuading them.
Ivor (*climbing the ladder*) How'd you mean? What's it to do with me?
Mr Quigley It's got to do with you, Ivor, because I'm planning to retire.
Ivor (*reaching up to the broken light*) Oh yes?
Mr Quigley And I'm confident I can fix it that you'll take over from me.
Ivor Really? But I get enough work being a handyman and that. I don't need a full-time job.
Mr Quigley Yes, you do, Ivor. Seen me through, this place, and it can see you through, an' all.

Ivor has by now taken out the bulb

Ivor Wonder if it's this...? (*He shakes the bulb*) No, that's all right. (*He puts the bulb back in and switches on a small torch to check where the wire meets the hanging shade*) Maybe it's the connection...
Mr Quigley (*not listening to Ivor*) Anyway, do you good having a sociable job like this.
Ivor What's that then, Dad?
Mr Quigley Lots of people come through this place, you know, Ivor. (*Roguishly*) Lots of young ladies...
Ivor Dad, I'm quite happy on my own.
Mr Quigley No, you're not. You been dead lonely since Janice died.
Ivor Maybe I have, but if I have, it's my business—all right?

Mr Quigley All right.

Pause

Got the aerobatics lot coming tonight. Some of them are quite tasty. And they strip down to them ... what're they called...? Leopards, that's right, leopards ... so at least you can see what you're getting.

Ivor Dad, I'm fine the way I am, thanks. Besides, it'd be a pretty peculiar woman who'd want to take on Ed and Kylie and Anneka.

Mr Quigley Ah, but women are peculiar, Ivor—that's part of their charm. Tell you, I once knew this totty——

Ivor I'm going up into the loft to check the connections.

During the ensuing dialogue, which is continuous, Ivor climbs down the ladder and moves it to the side of the stage. He then climbs up it as if going into some offstage attic area. (NB: the idea is that Ivor is in position to hear what happens in the next scene. If the theatre offers a lighting gallery or catwalk from which he can remain visible to the audience, that is ideal)

Mr Quigley (*recognising that this is a hint for him to shut up*) Right you are, then. (*He yawns and stretches*) Think I might just have a little snooze.

Mr Quigley goes in to his cubby-hole and closes the door behind him

Keith Horrobin enters from the DC entrance. He is still smartly dressed in his suit, but wearing a different shirt and tie. He looks quickly around the hall to see that there's no one about, then turns back to the entrance

Keith Lord Grevesham, please come through.

Lord Grevesham enters. In his sixties, a man of patrician looks and accent, he is wearing a smart evening dress, and almost, but not quite, has the relaxed manners of someone born to money and power. Keith behaves towards him with reverence bordering on sycophancy

Lord Grevesham Ah, thank you, Horrobin. (*He looks around the hall*) So this is the place.

Keith Yes.

Lord Grevesham Pretty run-down.

Keith As I said.

Lord Grevesham Hm. Some decisions'll have to be made about its future rather soon, I'd have thought.

Keith Exactly. I'm on the Village Hall Committee that makes those decisions.

Lord Grevesham And you feel confident you can see that such decisions go the right way?

Keith (*with a little smile*) No problem. That kind of committee doesn't attract the highest calibre of members.

Lord Grevesham No, I'm sure it doesn't. So one intelligent and motivated person in there...

Keith ...can ensure that he gets any decision that's required, yes.

Lord Grevesham Excellent. You're a good man, Horrobin.

Keith Thank you, my lord.

Lord Grevesham Call me Howard.

Keith (*very honoured*) Oh, thank you, Howard.

Lord Grevesham And what's your Christian name?

Keith Keith.

Lord Grevesham (*disappointedly*) Oh. Oh well, you can't have every-thing. (*He looks round the hall again*) The position's good. Need more car parking space, of course.

Keith There's the village football field.

Lord Grevesham Mm. What are the planners like round here?

Keith (*smugly*) Let's say I've got an "in" with the planning committee, Howard.

Lord Grevesham Good. Good. I must say I'm impressed with the way you organise your life ... Keith. The successful property business, the local council, the right committees...

Keith Thank you.

Lord Grevesham Remind me a bit of me when I was your age. You know, whatever you're doing, the most important skill is to be able to keep the different bits of your life in different compartments.

Keith I've always been very good at doing that.

Lord Grevesham Excellent. Because it's only when the walls between the compartments in your life break down that you get trouble. (*He moves across to look up at the grubby old lifebelt and shield on the back wall*) Any danger from conservation lobbies round here ... the loony left, the macrobiotic moaners, the pale-green do-gooders—they going to raise problems?

Keith Nothing we can't cope with. And a lot of people're going to be very glad to have a new Village Hall.

Lord Grevesham Particularly when it's only a car park's distance from a new superstore. Eh? (*He chuckles*)

Keith joins in the chuckling. They hear the DC *doors open and look towards them*

Tina comes busting in. She is the aerobics instructor, very busy and vigorous in all her movements. She is dressed in a garish sports shell suit over her leotard, and carries a sports bag

Lord Grevesham moves away to avoid participation in any conversation

Tina Evening.

Keith Good-evening.

Tina Haven't come for my aerobics class, have you?

Keith No.

Tina Pity. It's equally good for men as it is for women, you know.

Keith I'll take your word for it.

Tina (*moving to the* UR *exit*) Just going to get into my gear. Class starts prompt at seven.

Keith We'll be out by then.

Tina Brilliant.

She struts off through the UR *exit*

Lord Grevesham turns to face Keith and they both laugh

Lord Grevesham Had a Sergeant Major just like that when I did my National Service. He was prettier, mind.

Keith laughs sycophantically. Lord Grevesham looks around with satisfaction

So... I live in hopes of seeing this place knocked down and the foundations of the new superstore started within the year.

Keith I don't see why that shouldn't be possible, Howard.

Lord Grevesham Good man.

Keith (*delicately*) With regard to the other matter we discussed...

Lord Grevesham Hm?

Keith You were saying that, with the current MP nearing retirement, the local party would be looking for a suitable replacement candidate...

Lord Grevesham Yes, I remember.

Keith At the time you said you thought I might have certain qualities which would make me worthy of consideration...

Lord Grevesham Hm. Yes. And what I've heard from you this evening only reinforces that opinion ... Keith.

Keith (*to whom the world could offer little more*) Oh, thank you, Howard.

Lord Grevesham (*looking at his watch*) No time to discuss it now—due at this livery dinner. Maybe I could come and see you in your home environment...?

Keith Of course, Howard. Any time.

Lord Grevesham (*taking a diary out of his pocket*) Important to meet the wife and... You are happily married, aren't you, Keith?

Keith Blissfully.

Lord Grevesham (*checking in the diary*) Let's say Saturday week, six o'clock.

Keith Perfect. Would you care to stay for dinner? I'm sure Davina would be happy to——

Lord Grevesham Thank you, but no. Got a Lords Taverners shindig that evening.

Keith Ah.

Lord Grevesham Still, must be off. (*He looks at Keith appraisingly*) I think you could go a long way, Keith Horrobin ... if you play your cards right.

Keith Oh, don't worry, Howard. I'll play my cards right.

Davina and Candida enter through the DC *entrance. Davina, Keith's wife, is a few steps above him on the social ladder. (In fact, he married her largely for her class and money.) She is attractive and Sloaney, dressed in the Barbour appropriate to her class. Candida, the Horrobins' nearly-eight-year-old daughter, is a miniature clone of her mother, almost identically dressed. Davina is rushed and, as she comes in, does not notice Lord Grevesham*

Davina Keith, I noticed the Range Rover in the car park when I was driving back from Candida's ballet lesson.

Keith (*momentarily taken aback*) Oh. Davina. (*He recovers himself and comes forward to greet her effusively*) Darling, how lovely to see you.

He throws his arms round her and kisses her

Davina (*rather bewildered—she is not used to demonstrations of affection from her husband*) Keith...
Keith (*bending down to put his arms round Candida*) And how are you, my little gorgeous girl?

He gives her a little kiss on the nose

Candida (*as bewildered as her mother by this demonstration*) What are you doing, Daddy?
Keith Davina... Candida... I want you to meet a very important friend of mine... Lord Grevesham.
Lord Grevesham (*holding his hand out to Davina*) How do you do?
Davina (*shaking his hand*) A pleasure to meet you.
Lord Grevesham (*bending down to shake Candida's hand*) And how do you do, young lady?
Candida (*still a bit bewildered*) All right.
Lord Grevesham What a charming family you have, Keith.
Keith Oh, thank you.
Lord Grevesham Now, if you'll excuse me, I must be on my way. (*He smiles at Davina and Candida*) A pleasure to meet you both.
Davina (*automatically*) And you, Lord Grevesham.
Keith (*leading Lord Grevesham to the* DC *exit*) Let me see you to your car, Howard.
Lord Grevesham Thank you, Keith. So kind.

Keith and Lord Grevesham exit

Candida Mummy, why was Daddy so nice to us? What does he want?
Davina I don't know, Candida. But I'm sure we will know—very soon.

Keith comes bursting back into the hall, extremely angry

Keith Now, just what the hell are you up to, Davina? Are you spying on me? That was a very important business meeting I was having.
Davina I just saw the car and I needed to talk to you. Since you leave so early and get home so late, I have to grab my chances when I can.
Keith Well, don't ever appear unannounced again. You could ruin everything.

Davina And what is "everything", may I ask?

Keith Mind your own business.

Candida That's more like the Daddy I know.

Keith Shut up, you little brat!

Candida So's that.

Keith (*looking at his watch*) I've got to be off at another meeting in a moment. What was it you wanted?

Davina I wanted to talk to you about Candida's birthday.

Keith Oh, for heaven's sake, Davina! Can't you do anything on your own? Just go out and buy her something. It's not as if we haven't got the money.

Davina It's not as if I haven't got the money.

Keith is momentarily abashed by this

Anyway, it's not her present. That's been decided.

Candida I'm going to have a pony.

Keith You've already got a pony.

Candida I'm going to have a bigger pony.

Davina I wanted to talk about her party.

Keith When's that?

Davina On her birthday, of course. Her birthday happens to fall on a Saturday this year, so that's when she'll have her party.

Keith When is it?

Davina Saturday week. The nineteenth.

Keith Well, that's... Oh no, Saturday week won't do. We'll have to change the date.

Candida Look, I've had the same birthday for the last seven years, and I'm not going to change it now.

Keith Not the date of the birthday, the date of the party, you little idiot.

Davina Why can't we do Saturday week?

Keith Because that is when Lord Grevesham is coming to see me at the house in the middle of my happy family life.

Davina I'd have thought a children's party was a perfect demonstration of happy family life.

Keith Not with Candida and her friends it isn't. When they get together they're like St Trinian's crossed with the Hezbollah.

Davina Keith, can't you put Lord Grevesham off? I've promised Candida that——

Keith No, I cannot put Lord Grevesham off. You have no idea what's at stake here.

Davina I might have some idea if you ever told me what was going on in your life.

Keith Listen, all you need to know at the moment is that you cannot give a party for Candida in our house on Saturday week. (*He moves to the downstage exit*) Now, if you'll excuse me...

Davina Will you be back late?

Keith (*as he goes out through the door*) Yes!

Keith exits

Davina stands for a moment, tense, then suddenly starts to cry. She reaches into her pocket for a handkerchief. The broken light comes on, though Davina and Candida do not notice it. Ivor descends the ladder back on to the stage

Candida Crying doesn't help.

Davina No, no, I know it doesn't, but ... (*She wipes her nose determinedly with her handkerchief*) it's a relief.

She sees Ivor standing thunderstruck at the foot of the ladder, looking at her as if he's never seen anything so beautiful in his entire life. Davina sniffs briskly to cover her crying and puts away her handkerchief

Good-evening.

Ivor (*dumbly*) Good-evening.

Candida (*matter-of-factly*) I'd divorce Daddy if I was you.

Davina (*with a half-laugh, moving towards the downstage exit*) On what grounds?

Candida (*as they go out*) Take your pick. Mental cruelty, certainly. Unreasonable behaviour. Probably adultery too, if I know him...

Davina and Candida exit

Ivor dumbly watches them go out. He stands for a moment, lost in troubled thought

Georgina and Paula Hewlett come in through the DC entrance. They are wearing outdoor coats and carry sports bags

Ivor looks up to see them enter

Georgina Come along, Paula. The class starts at seven.
Paula I'm here, Mummy. (*Seeing Ivor, she deliberately drops her sports bag, spilling towels, leotard, shampoo, etc.*) Oh, sorry. Won't be a moment.
Georgina For heaven's sake, Paula. (*She goes to the changing rooms* UR) Hurry up, girl.

Georgina exits

Paula Just coming. (*She turns to Ivor as soon as Georgina's out of sight. She whispers urgently*) You're Ed's dad, aren't you?
Ivor 'Sright.
Paula Well, Mr Quigley, I wonder, would you mind please——

She takes a letter surreptitiously out of her bag and thrusts it into Ivor's hands

—giving him this.

Paula scurries off after her mother

Ivor No, that'd be… (*Seeing that she is gone, he puts the letter into his pocket*) Dad was right. They are peculiar. (*He moves towards the* UL *entrance*) Better see if the lights in the big hall're working.

He goes off

Patti, her friend Kelly, and other members of the aerobics class, including Henrietta, a rather large and excitable young girl, come in through the DC *entrance. All the others go through to the changing rooms* UR, *but Patti and Kelly begin to remove their coats and jumpers to reveal that they are wearing brightly coloured leotards and tights underneath. They talk from the moment they come in through the doors*

During their dialogue, Tina, Amazonian in her own brightly-coloured leotard, emerges from the changing rooms UR, *carrying a cassette player. She puts the box down and plugs the cassette player into a socket* C *stage*

Patti ...and I said, "Well, it's all right for you. You don't have to share an office with her all day." Janet wasn't best pleased about that, Kelly, I can tell you.

Kelly I bet she wasn't.

Patti And then Roger came in—as usual getting the timing just wrong— and he made a joke—also very ill-timed—about Janet's blouse.

Kelly Which one was she wearing, Patti—her beige with the little yellow flowers?

Patti No, Kelly, the blue one with the thin stripe. Together with that navy tight skirt with the buttons.

Kelly I know. So what did Roger say?

Patti He said, "Which are the non-smoking seats, hostess?" Well, you can imagine Janet's reaction to that.

Kelly I certainly can.

By this point Patti and Kelly have got their outer garments off and are down to their leotards

Tina Henrietta, could you get the steps out, please.

During the ensuing dialogue, Georgina and Paula, together with the other members of the class, all dressed in brightly-coloured leotards, come out of the changing rooms and stand around, stretching and limbering up

Also during the dialogue, Henrietta, enthusiastic as ever, with the help of other members of the class, brings on the aerobic steps. They set out as many of them as there are members of the group on the floor in rows. Henrietta sets one separately down stage for Tina. As soon as she has given her orders to Henrietta, Tina goes across to join Patti and Kelly

Tina Came in your leotards, I see.

Patti Yes.

Tina Why, aren't you expecting to sweat?

Patti Not that much, no.

Tina I'll see to it you do sweat. No pain—no gain, Patti.

Patti No sweat—no fret, Tina.

Tina (*with a beady look at Patti*) I hope you two haven't just come here to gossip, as usual.

Kelly Would we?

Georgina comes across to join Tina, dragging a rather unwilling Paula with her

Georgina Tina, I'd like to introduce my daughter Paula.
Tina Brilliant to meet you. First-timers always welcome.
Paula Thank you.
Tina Why haven't we seen you here before?
Georgina (*forbiddingly*) Because she's been occupying her evenings in other, less suitable ways. I'm now going to see to it that I know about everything Paula gets up to in her spare time.

Paula gives her mother a sullen look. Henrietta comes bubbling across to Tina

Henrietta All the steps're out, Tina.
Tina Brilliant, Henrietta. Raring to go, are you?
Henrietta Oh, absolutely raring.
Tina Brilliant.
Henrietta One thing, could I ask you, Tina...?
Tina Mm?
Henrietta Erm, well, I've been coming to these classes now for seven weeks, and I think you once said that step aerobics burns up ninety per cent of body fat.
Tina Yes.
Henrietta So why haven't I lost any weight?
Tina Because you're not trying hard enough, Henrietta.
Henrietta Oh. Oh dear.
Tina (*clapping her hands*) Right, now could you all get ready, please. (*She crosses to the cassette player*) And we'll start as usual with a warm-up—just a march—in time to the music. (*She switches on the cassette player*) And go! With shoulder gyrations too!

The music starts. Tina leads the class in a circle round the steps in the middle. They march vigorously, moving their shoulders up and down with their hands on top of them. All are in step, except for Henrietta, who is marching enthusiastically out of step, moving her shoulders out of rhythm—though she doesn't realise she's doing it wrong. Paula goes along unwillingly behind her mother. Patti and Kelly start talking again the minute they start walking

Patti You see, what Roger didn't know was that Janet actually used to be an air-hostess.

Kelly Really? I didn't know that either.

Patti Yes. On Virgin. Which, given Janet, couldn't have been less appropriate. But clearly, she thought Roger did know and was just getting at her, and so she said, "At least I never sold double glazing for a living".

Kelly Why, did he?

Patti Yes.

Kelly I didn't know that.

Tina (*stopping the march*) And that's enough.

They all stop. Patti and Kelly also stop, but continue talking, not aware that everyone else is looking at them

Patti Oh yes, had a very chequered past, our Roger. When he was in his twenties, he suddenly took off to Nepal to find himself.

Kelly And did he?

Patti What?

Kelly Find himself?

Patti Oh no. When he finally got to Nepal, he found he'd just left.

Kelly Oh.

By this time they are aware that everyone is looking at them

Tina When you've *quite* finished... We are meant to be here for a serious aerobics class. Now, could you move to your boxes, please.

The class move into position, each in front of one of the steps. Patti and Kelly, taking up positions by adjacent steps, start talking again

I'm going to separate you two. Henrietta—change places with Kelly.

Henrietta does so, beaming. Kelly is now some way away from Patti

And we'll start ... leading with the right.

The class follow Tina's movements in time with her and the music—all except for Henrietta, who is completely out of time with the others. Patti

once again starts talking—calling across the room to Kelly—as soon as
Tina starts the exercise

Once the aerobic class is established, with Tina shouting her orders, the
class—except for Henrietta—following them together, Patti and Kelly
gossiping, there occurs the theatrical equivalent of a radio fade. The
Lights slowly dim, the volume of the music and the voices goes down in
time with them, until the stage is in total darkness and total silence

Step—and two—and three—and four—and five—and six—and seven—
and eight! Now leading with the left. Step—and two—and three—and
four—and five—and six—and seven—and eight! And now let's do it
with the arms swinging. Basic marching movement with the arms. And
repeat, leading with the right. Step—and two—and three—and four—
and five—and six—and seven—and eight!, etc.

Patti So, anyway, Janet just turned on Roger and said, "Don't imagine for
a moment I've forgotten about that business with the photocopier!"

Kelly I shouldn't think anyone's forgotten that.

Patti No. I was surprised the photocopier didn't break under the weight.

Kelly Maybe some of the lads held him over it.

Patti I'd've thought you'd need the downwards pressure to get a sharp
image, though.

Kelly Well, it certainly was a sharp image. Funny, I'd never thought of
him having moles *there*.

Patti No. Wouldn't have been a surprise to Janet, though.

Kelly What—you mean he and she…? I didn't know…

Scene 3

Everything from the previous scene has been struck. The calendar now
reads "Wednesday 9th". Some chairs have been set round the edges of the
central acting area

The F.A.D.S. are rehearsing Julius Caesar. *In the tape-marked area of the*
floor, Lydia is playing Portia to Rod's Brutus. Rod is ideally very tall and
in his twenties, far too young to be matched with Lydia. He is extremely
embarrassed by the overt sexuality of her acting. They are dressed in
normal clothes, though Lydia's rig-out is markedly more bohemian than

that which she wore for the committee meeting. She has on a low-cut blouse and a wrap-around skirt. Though very full of herself, Lydia is not a bad actress. Rod is a very gawky, effete and ineffectual actor. What's more, he doesn't yet know the lines, and reads laboriously from a Penguin copy of the play—behind which he hides from Lydia's more obvious advances

They are watched by the director of Julius Caesar, *Martyn Graves. He is in his fifties, dressed in studiedly casual clothes, with a patterned scarf tied round his neck. He holds open—but does not look at—a ring-file, in which he has pages from the Penguin edition of* Julius Caesar *pasted on to A4 sheets*

Also present is Benji Sparrow, a good-looking actor in his thirties, who believes himself to be God's gift to everything. He sits doing a crossword, studiously taking no notice of the scene that's being rehearsed

Veronica, the nervous, bespectacled prompter, sits hunched over a copy of the text. A few other cast members—including Ed, a good-looking, smallish sixteen-year-old—sit around the edge of the rehearsal space, but there aren't many of them—there's a flu epidemic

As the action starts, Lydia launches herself at Rod and throws her arms round him. He is somewhat confused by the sudden assault

Lydia   "Dear my lord,
                   Make me acquainted with your cause of grief."
Rod (*reading slowly and without fluency*) "I am not well in health, and
                   that is all."
Lydia   "Brutus is wise, and were he not in health,
                   He would

She tightens her embrace on Rod, much to his discomfiture

                            embrace the means to come by it."
Rod   "Why, so I do. Good Portia, go to bed."

Lydia nods enthusiastically, takes Rod by the hand and starts to lead him off stage. He resists. Lydia stops and looks at him in disappointment

Lydia   "Is Brutus sick. And is it physical
To add unto his sickness? No, my Brutus;
You have some sick offence within your mind,
Which, by the right and virtue of my place,
I ought to know of; and,

She glides down to the floor, still with her arms around the bemused Rod

upon my knees,
I charm you, by my once commended beauty,
By all your vows of love,

She tightens her arms around his knees, so that Rod almost loses his balance

and that great vow
Which did incorporate and make us one, (*She pauses*)
That you unfold to me, (*She takes a longer pause*) your
self…" (*She takes an even longer dramatic pause*)

Veronica (*prompting*) "Your half——"
Lydia (*venomously*) Shut up, Veronica, that was acting!
Veronica (*in a little, crestfallen voice*) Sorry.
Lydia (*very dramatically*)   "…your half,
Why you are heavy."
Rod (*almost falling over*) "Kneel not, gentle Portia."
Lydia   "I should not need, if you were gentle, Brutus.
Within the bond of marriage, tell me, Brutus,
Is it excepted, I should know no secrets
That appertain to you? Am I your self
But, as it were, in sort of limitation,
To keep with you at meals,

She suddenly moves up Rod's body, still with her arms around him, so that her face is very close to his

comfort your bed, (*She puckers her lips as if expecting a
kiss. She doesn't get one, which makes her slightly
miffed*)
And talk to you sometimes? Dwell I but in the suburbs

Of your good pleasure? If it be no more,
Portia is Brutus' *harlot, (She suddenly pulls apart the top
of her blouse, drawing attention to her cleavage)* not
his wife."

Rod *(gulping with embarrassment)* "You are my true and honourable
wife,
As dear to me as are the ruddy drops
That visit my sad heart."

Lydia   "If this were true then should I know this secret. (*She runs
her arms slinkily down her sides*)
I grant I am a *woman*; but withal
A woman well-reputed, Cato's daughter.
Think you I am no stronger than my
(*She thrusts herself against him*)   *sex*,
Being so father'd, and so husbanded?
Tell me your counsels, I will not disclose 'em.
I have made strong proof of my constancy,
Giving myself a voluntary wound (*She suddenly flicks
open her skirt to reveal her thigh*)
Here, in the thigh; can I bear that with patience,
And not my husband's secrets?"

She once again wraps herself around Rod

Rod *(in heartfelt embarrassment)* "Oh, ye gods,
Render me worthy of this noble wife!"

He manages, with some difficulty, to disentangle himself from Lydia

Veronica *(in a little mousy voice)* "Knock, knock."
Martyn Don't interrupt, Veronica. I said we'd run this straight through.
Veronica I'm not interrupting, Martyn. (*She points to the text*) That's
what it says. "Knocking within."
Martyn Oh, all right. (*To the actors*) Go on.
Rod   "Hark, hark! one knocks."
Veronica *(self-righteously)* See!
Rod   "Portia, go in awhile;
And by and by thy bosom shall partake
The secrets of my heart.

Lydia throws herself once again at Rod, and starts kissing him passionately. He manages, again with difficulty, to break free

Leave me with haste.

Rather disconsolately, Lydia moves to the side of the stage. At the edge of the acting area, she turns and blows a passionate kiss to Rod. With relief, he turns to look off the other way

Lucius, who's that knocks?"

There is a silence. No one reacts

Martyn Lucius! Where the hell's Lucius?
Veronica He's got flu.
Martyn Oh God, not another one. I'm sure Peter Hall doesn't have this trouble.
Veronica I could read Lucius in if you like, Martyn.
Martyn No, we're not reduced to that.

Veronica looks hurt, even a little tearful. Martyn does not notice but addresses Lydia and Rod

Just a few points arising from the scene, loves. You've been doing a bit of private work on it, haven't you, Lydia?
Lydia Yes. Well, I thought it was important to bring out Portia's physical side.
Martyn I think you can rest assured that you did that.
Lydia I mean, she is a *woman.*
Martyn Undoubtedly.
Lydia With her own identity. With her own *sexuality.* I think it's very important that comes out.
Martyn Yes. Of course, at the same time she is an aristocratic Roman lady. Cato's daughter and all that. So I wonder if maybe we were getting a teensiest bit too much of the physicality...?
Lydia I think it's essential to establish that Brutus and Portia's marriage is strong sexually.
Martyn Yes, I agree, love, but perhaps not quite *that* strong. I mean, anyway, it will be different when you're in the cozzies.
Lydia Why?

Martyn Well, the physical stuff's not going to register much with you all muffled up in a dressing gown, is it?

Lydia But I'm not going to be all muffled up in a dressing gown.

Martyn Oh? What did you reckon you'd be wearing, then?

Lydia Well, an off-the-shoulder, low-cut backless gown. White. I got it for a Masonic Ladies Night of Bernard's last winter. It was described in the shop as "Grecian-style". Be perfect. And it's got a slit up the side, so I can do the thigh biz.

Martyn Yes, I was a bit concerned about the thigh biz.

Lydia (*affronted*) Why?

Martyn Well, it's the class thing again. Back to Cato's daughter. Respectable Roman matron and all that.

Lydia Portia is not a matron. She's only about ... well, the age I'm playing her.

Benji (*taking an interest in the proceedings for the first time*) And what age is that, love?

Lydia Sort of ... thirtyish.

Benji Oh, I see. A character part. (*He returns to his crossword*)

Lydia shoots a venomous look at him

Martyn Erm ... going back to the thigh biz, Lydia love.

Lydia Mm? ·

Martyn The "voluntary wound". I'm not sure that showing so much leg is quite——

Lydia But she's got to show her leg. She makes a point of saying "Giving myself a voluntary wound/*Here* in the thigh". Why does she say "here", if she's not showing it?

Martyn (*losing ground*) Maybe she's——

Lydia I think it's terribly important that the audience should see it.

Martyn (*rather anxiously*) See the "voluntary wound"?

Lydia Yes.

Martyn (*even more anxiously*) But... I mean... What kind of "voluntary wound" did you actually have in mind, Lydia love?

Lydia (*taking Rod's copy of the play from him to show her textual research*) Ah, now I've looked at the text in some detail and I've worked out exactly what Shakespeare meant.

Martyn Really?

Lydia Think about it... What kind of voluntary wound does a woman give herself to show love for a man?

Martyn Well, it's not something that happens very often nowadays, but I suppose in Roman times——

Lydia But it does happen often nowadays. Lots of girls do it.

Martyn Do what?

Lydia (*triumphantly*) Have themselves tattooed.

Martyn Tattooed? Are you suggesting Portia's "voluntary wound" is a tattoo?

Lydia Yes. Obviously that's what Shakespeare meant. It's in the text.

Benji suddenly bursts out laughing

And what are you finding so funny, Benji?

Benji (*laughing*) Just the idea of a tattoo. What will it be—a great big heart with a dagger through it and a scroll reading "Portia loves Brutus"?

Lydia No, of course it won't!

Martyn (*trying to head off confrontation*) Hm. Well, perhaps we should discuss the tattoo later, in the pub.

Benji (*looking at his watch*) Oh yes, nearly drinkies time, isn't it?

Martyn Yes. So we'd better move along, luvvies.

Rod Er … any notes for me?

Martyn What?

Rod On the scene. Any notes for Brutus?

Martyn Oh. Right. Erm… I'm sorry, Rod love, I'm afraid I was so mesmerised by what Lydia was doing I hardly noticed you.

Lydia smiles, gratified by what she takes as a compliment

Erm, yes, well, actually that is a note. Could you make your Brutus a bit more conspicuous?

Rod More conspicuous?

Martyn Yes, give him more ooomph.

Rod More ooomph, right. (*He looks totally confused*)

Benji Thing I found, actually, Rod, when I was giving my Brutus for the Hensley Histrionics, was it helped to play that scene as if it was very cold.

Rod What, the weather?

Benji Yes. Do a bit of shivering, rubbing your arms, you know … may help you get more of the feeling of it.

Rod Oh.

Benji Just a tip. Hope you don't mind my passing it on, Martyn...?

Martyn No, no, anything that helps, Benji.

Benji Well, it certainly worked for me. Do you know, the Hensley Gazette described my Brutus as "a profoundly moving study of wounded dignity".

Lydia (*unimpressed*) "Wounded dignity".

Benji (*coming back at her*) Yes. Though no doubt you'd think of it as "tattooed dignity", Lydia.

Lydia (*turning on him in fury*) Now listen, Benji, I'm not——

Martyn Please, please. We've got a lot to do. Open in less than a fortnight, luvvies, don't forget.

Disgruntled, Lydia goes to sit down and starts reading a magazine

Oh yes, Tuesday week we've all got to be on the green D.L.P.

Veronica (*bewildered*) "On the green"? I thought we were doing it in the theatre.

Martyn Oh, sorry, luvvy. The "green" is what people in the business call the stage.

Veronica Oh.

Martyn And "D.L.P." I'm sure you know.

Veronica looks blank

Dead Letter Perfect.

Veronica (*still looking blank*) Oh.

Benji Means knowing your lines.

Veronica Ah.

Martyn Don't worry, Veronica, you'll catch on soon enough. When you've done a few more productions for the F.A.D.S.

Veronica Yes. Do you think there's a chance I might get a part in the next production? I mean, I have prompted for the last eleven.

Martyn (*dismissively*) Yes, well, we'll have to think about that. Now, what was I going to move on to next?

Benji You said you wanted to choreograph the battle scenes tonight.

Martyn Yes, but I can't do that without my bloody armies, can I? I called all the soldiers for tonight and look—none of them are here.

Ed stands up. Martyn does not notice him

Ed Erm...

Veronica It's the flu.

Martyn Honestly! Here I am trying to create a work of art and I'm frustrated at every turn. When on earth am I going to choreograph those battle scenes?

Benji Be time Saturday week, when we do the first Dress Rehearsal, won't there?

Martyn There'll have to be. Oh dear. I want those battle scenes to be vast pageants of movement, an impression of teeming hordes of war-crazed men billowing across the stage.

Ed Er... I'm here, Mr Graves.

Martyn What?

Ed I'm one of the soldiers.

Martyn Oh. Hardly a teeming horde of war-crazed men, are you?

Ed Sorry about that.

Martyn Which one are you?

Ed Ed Quigley.

Martyn Oh, really? Ivor's boy.

Ed 'Sright. He said you need a few extra bods, so I come along.

Martyn Yes.

Ed (*gloomily*) Well, I sort of ... got time on my hands at the moment.

Martyn Ivor isn't around, by any chance, this evening, is he? I thought he said he'd drop in to talk through the sound cues.

Ed Yes, he's here. He's watching the football with my grandad.

Martyn Oh.

Ed Shall I get him?

Martyn If you wouldn't mind...

Ed No sweat.

Ed crosses to the door of Mr Quigley's cubby-hole and knocks

Mr Quigley (*off*) Come in.

During Benji's speech that follows, Ed goes into the cubby-hole: a short burst of television football commentary is heard while the door is open

Benji If you're really going to have hordes of war-crazed men for the battles, Martyn, it's going to be hellishly crowded in the wings. I mean, remember the chaos backstage when we did *Henry V*. (*He turns to*

Veronica with sudden charm) As a matter of fact, Veronica, the Frinsley Advertiser, no less, described my Henry as "a performance that'd put many professionals to shame".

Veronica (*impressed*) Oh?

Benji (*smugly*) Thought you'd like to know that.

Martyn Actually, Benji, I have devised a way round the wing space problem.

Benji Oh?

Martyn (*moving across to* R *to illustrate his words*) You see, we'll open these two doors behind the stage and then when the soldiers are coming on and off they can come round this way. And then we'll have the P.A. relayed through here so that people can hear their cues.

Benji Splendid. How many soldiers are you actually going to have, Martyn?

Martyn Many as I can get.

Benji You know, when I gave my Coriolanus for the Depton Drama Club, we had symbolic armies. One person represented all the Roman army and another one was all the Volsces.

Martyn Oh. Well, you know I hate gimmicky productions.

Benji Actually, you know, Veronica, The Depton Chronicle said my Coriolanus was "heart-rendingly aloof."

Veronica (*impressed*) Oh?

Martyn I'm also going to use a rather clever trick to make the armies look bigger.

Benji (*joking*) What—have them carry branches of trees like in The Scottish Play?

Martyn No, no.

Veronica What's the Scottish Play?

Benji A certain play by one W. Shakespeare about a thane who kills the king and takes over his throne.

Veronica Oh, you mean *Macb——*

Both Benji and Martyn leap on her and put hands over her mouth

Martyn Don't ever do that again! Not in any theatre I'm working in— please!

Veronica (*when they've removed their hands*) Why? What did I do?

Benji Don't you know it's bad luck?

Veronica What is?

Martyn To mention...
Veronica What? Oh, you mean to mention *Macb*——

*Once again Martyn and Benji hurl themselves across the stage to gag her.
After a moment, cautiously, giving her grave looks of warning, they
remove their hands*

(*In a very little voice*) Sorry.
Martyn Don't worry. You'll learn. (*He is suddenly magnanimous*) Had
a thought, Veronica love. You *can* have a part.
Veronica An acting part?
Martyn Yes. In *Julius Caesar.*
Veronica (*terribly over-excited*) Ooh. Who will I be?
Martyn You'll be one of the soldiers.
Veronica (*still excited*) Oh. Martyn. Thank you.
Benji Aren't people going to notice that one of the soldiers is a woman?
Martyn No, no. They'll be in armour.
Veronica (*excited*) Ooh.
Martyn Totally unrecognizable. Which is how I'm going to do my trick
to make the armies look bigger.
Benji What is the trick?
Martyn (*very pleased with himself*) I'm going to have the same actors
playing both armies.
Benji Won't the audience notice that?
Martyn (*breezily*) No, no. The two sides'll have different coloured
banners. And we'll have as many as possible. Teeming war-crazed
hordes. Everyone I can dragoon in. (*An idea comes to him*) Ooh, Lydia
love—as Portia, you'll be dead by then, won't you?
Lydia (*affronted*) Are you suggesting that I should be one of the soldiers?
Martyn Yes.
Lydia (*with crushing dignity*) Lydia Millington doesn't double, Martyn.
Martyn Oh.

The door from Mr Quigley's cubby-hole opens

Ivor and Ed come out. Ivor is holding a copy of the Penguin edition of
Julius Caesar

Ivor Evening, Mr Graves. You wanted to talk about the sound cues?

Martyn Oh yes, Ivor, I did. Have you read through the play?
Ivor Most of it. Funny language, isn't it?
Martyn But did all the sound cues I'd marked up make sense?
Ivor Yeah, most of them. 'Cept there's one thing kept cropping up and I don't know what it is.
Martyn What was that?
Ivor "Allerum".
Martyn "Allerum"?
Ivor Keeps coming up towards the end.
Martyn Show me.

Ivor points to something in his script

Oh, "alarum". It's "alarum", Ivor.
Ivor (*as if he understands*) Oh, alarum, right. (*He pauses*) What's an alarum then?
Martyn It's a fanfare.
Ivor Oh, OK, got you. No problem.
Benji (*looking at his watch*) Martyn, are we going to be doing more rehearsal, because it's nearly ten?
Martyn Oh, is it? Well, we mustn't miss out on our drinking time, must we?
Benji First things first, after all.
Martyn Yes, luvvies, we'd better break it there. Continue talking it through in the *Queen's Head*—OK?
Benji Right.
Rod Fine. Must just go and have a pee.

Rod goes off UR

The other cast members gather coats together, etc. and start to wander off out through the DC *exit*

Ivor and Ed go to get their coats

Ivor You seem a bit down in the dumps, son. What is it?
Ed Oh. You know... Paula doesn't want to see me any more.
Ivor Sorry. That what she wrote in her letter, was it?
Ed What letter?

Ivor Well, the one that... (*He thinks for a moment*) 'Ere, didn't I give it
you? (*He reaches into his pocket and takes out Paula's letter*)

*Ed snatches the letter out of his hand, tears open the envelope and hastily
reads it. Ivor looks on in some bemusement*

Ed (*ecstatically*) Fantastic! She's going to be able to get to the end of
Youth Club tomorrow. Yeah!

*He leaps in the air and punches upwards, turns a cartwheel and rushes
off* DC

Ivor (*following him somewhat more slowly and still bewildered*) Good
news, was it then, son?

He exits

*Veronica picks up a cardboard box from under her chair and brings it
proudly across to Martyn. By now Martyn has got his coat on and is about
to leave*

Martyn What's this, love?
Veronica (*simpering sycophantically*) The programmes. You know, I got
the copy together last week and took it to the printers ... and I went down
after work today and picked them up ... and here they are.
Martyn Oh, bless you, Veronica. Let's have a look.

*She lifts the lid of the box for him, and Martyn takes out an unfolded
programme from the top of the pile. He looks at the text and then suddenly
becomes furious*

Oh, good heavens! (*He puts a dramatically pained hand to his fore-
head*) This is the end—the absolute end!
Veronica (*very anxiously*) What's the matter?
Martyn (*pointing furiously to something in the text*) Look at that! I mean,
will you just look at that!
Veronica I can't see what——
Martyn It's spelt with an "i"! You've spelt it with an "i"! Just like any
common or garden little "Martin". I am Martyn with a "y"! Oh, for

heaven's sake, what will the audience think? They'll come into the theatre expecting a "Martyn Graves Production", and they'll look in the programme and think they've come to the wrong place! I should think half of them would just walk out on the spot!

Veronica I'm sorry...

Martyn "Sorry" is not enough! This is an absolute disaster! (*He sweeps down stage*) I'm going now, and I'll have to think very seriously about whether or not I come back! (*He stalks off to the* DC *exit*) I think it very possible that the F.A.D.S. production of *Julius Caesar* will have to start looking for another director!

He exits, majestically furious

Veronica (*in tears*) Oh, Martyn! Martyn!

She scuttles off after him

Lydia (*casually looking after Martyn*) I was thinking we hadn't had one of his little tantrums for a while.

Benji No. (*With a dramatic sigh, as he goes to get his coat*) Oh well, I'd better go down to the *Queen's Head* and start pouring whisky on to his ruffled feathers.

Lydia How do you think the show's going, Benji?

Benji (*with a shrug*) As you'd expect. Some bits're good—the bits I'm in. The bits Rod is in are frankly dreadful. (*He moves towards the* DC *exit*) Still, unfortunately, there's no way I can play Mark Antony *and* Brutus ... so I'm afraid we're stuck with it. You going for a drink?

Lydia Be with you shortly.

Benji (*going out*) See you.

Benji exits

Lydia is now alone on stage. All the others have gone. She crosses to Mr Quigley's cubby-hole and knocks on the door

Mr Quigley opens it

Mr Quigley All done?

Lydia Pretty well.

Mr Quigley (*looking at his watch*) Right, I'd better be——
Lydia If you don't want to miss your drink, Mr Quigley, give me the keys
and I'll lock up for you.
Mr Quigley Oh, that's very kind of you, Mrs Millington. Just get my coat.
(*He produces his coat, which he's clearly been holding behind his back*)

*He locks the cubby-hole quickly and hands the keys to Lydia. He starts
putting his coat on as he moves speedily towards the DC exit*

Lydia I'll bring them to you in the snug before closing time.
Mr Quigley Bless you, Mrs Millington. (*He moves to the DC exit*) See you
shortly, then.

Mr Quigley exits

Lydia (*calling after him*) Right you are. (*She moves across to the cubby-
hole and unlocks it*)

Rod emerges from the UR entrance

Lydia turns to see him. She leans provocatively in the doorway

Rod...
Rod Mm?
Lydia There's something in here I'd like to show you.
Rod Oh?

*Curious, he moves across to the door. Lydia goes inside out of sight. Rod
stands by the door. Lydia's arm reaches out. She grabs his hand and yanks
him quickly inside. There is a little strangled gulp from Rod, as Lydia uses
her foot to shut the door behind them*

Black-out

SCENE 4

*The calendar reads "Thursday 10th". The coat-hanging area UR is now
adorned with a lot of young people's anoraks, baseball jackets, school*

bags, etc. A table with soft drink bottles and plastic beakers has been set up stage

Against this sits the Revd Elkins, strumming a guitar. He is dressed very casually—not a trace of a dog collar in sight—and is being unctuously informal and secular to his Youth Club members. These sit around him on the floor, the younger ones singing along enthusiastically to the chorus of the song, the older ones looking bored and rebellious. Among the keen younger ones is an earnest and bespectacled girl called Tracey. Among the bored older ones are Ed, Charlie and Dan. The last two are big seventeen-year-old public school types who think the world owes them a living. Dan in particular really reckons he's Mr Cool

The sound starts in darkness, as the Revd Elkins strums away. (He is not a very good guitarist—or come to that, a very good singer—but he makes up for this in hearty and off-putting bonhomie)

The Lights slowly come up to reveal the scene

Revd Elkins (*singing*) Michael row the boat ashore.
All (*with varying degrees of enthusiasm*) Al—le—lu—u—ya.
Revd Elkins   Michael row the boat ashore.
All   Al—le—lu—u—ya.
Revd Elkins   Sister helped to trim the sail.
All   Al—le—lu—u—ya.
Revd Elkins   Sister helped to trim the sail.
All   Al—le—lu—u—ya.
Revd Elkins   The river Jordan is chilly and cold.
All   Al—le—lu—u—ya.
Revd Elkins (*getting what he imagines to be more ethnic and West Indian as he gets further into the song*) Chills de body, but not de soul.
All   Al—le—lu—u—ya.
Revd Elkins   De ribber Jordan am deep and wide.
All   Al—le—lu—u—ya.
Revd Elkins   Milk and honey on de udder side.
All   Al—le—lu—u—ya.
Revd Elkins   And again! (*He does an elaborate closing strum on the guitar*)

All (*slowing right down*) Al—le—lu—u—ya!
Revd Elkins There, that was a jolly song, wasn't it?

The older kids' expressions show just how jolly they think it was

Tracey (*very enthusiastically*) Yes, it was great.
Revd Elkins And, you know, as well as being a terrific tune, the song's got some messages for all of us in its words. Any idea what those messages might be?

Blank silence from all present

Oh, come on. Now I know our Youth Club evenings are nothing to do with religion, they're just occasions when we can all gather together and have a jolly good time, but, you know, God has a little habit of getting in everywhere. Yes, even when you're—(*he swings his arms in a rather embarrassing way, imitating what he imagines to be dance movements*) "bopping in a funky way at your disco", God's watching you.
Dan (*under his breath*) Bloody hope He isn't.

Charlie and the other older ones giggle

Revd Elkins Sorry, Dan, didn't catch that.
Dan Nothing, RevJim.
Revd Elkins Well, come on—anyone got any ideas about the message in the words of the song?
Tracey Well, RevJim... That bit "Sister helped to trim the sail..."
Revd Elkins Yes, great. What do you think that means, Tracey?
Tracey Well, I think it means, probably ... that Michael's sister ... helped Michael ... to trim the sail.
Revd Elkins Super. Jolly good. Well done, Tracey. Anything else it tells any of you? (*He looks around hopefully*)

None of them respond

Well, what about the "milk and honey" on the other side of "de ribber Jordan"...? Does anyone know who's going to be getting some of that milk and honey?
Tracey (*tentatively*) Michael...?

Revd Elkins Yes, Tracey—excellent. And why do you think Michael's going to get some milk and honey?

Tracey Erm… (*She thinks about this*) Is it because he's got a sore throat…?

Revd Elkins I beg your pardon?

Tracey Well, when I get a sore throat, my mum always does me hot milk with honey.

Revd Elkins Yes, but——

Tracey And Michael might have got a sore throat 'cause "de ribber Jordan is chilly and cold", so maybe it's gone on to his chest…

Dan and Charlie and some of the older ones start giggling at this. The Revd Elkins changes tack once again to stop them

Revd Elkins Yes. Jolly interesting idea, Tracey. (*Enthusiastically*) Well, now, what do we all want to do for the rest of the evening?

Dan (*under his breath to Charlie*) Get Katie out into the car park.

Charlie and the older girls giggle

Revd Elkins Sorry, Dan, did you say something?

Dan No, RevJim. Not a dicky-bird.

Revd Elkins Oh. Well, remember, Dan, God not only sees everything we do—He also hears everything we say. *And* He even listens in to everything we're thinking.

Dan (*again under his breath*) Bloody nosey, isn't He?

Charlie and the older girls giggle

Revd Elkins (*clearing his throat pointedly*) All I'm saying is that, wherever we may be, at any moment, God can suddenly be with us.

The doors to the hatch from the "Sydney Pratt Memorial Room" suddenly open to reveal Mr Quigley framed in them

Dan Oh, hallo, God.

Revd Elkins (*angrily*) Now, Dan——

Mr Quigley (*talking to someone out of sight behind him*) And this here's the serving hatch … you know, for serving food and what-have-you.

(*He sees the vicar*) Evening, your reverence. Just showing someone round the premises.

Revd Elkins Oh, right. We going to be in your way?

Mr Quigley Well, be simpler if you could just slip into the Sydney Pratt for quarter of an hour or so, if you don't mind.

Revd Elkins No problem.

Mr Quigley closes the hatch doors and disappears out of sight

OK, chaps and chapesses, we'll continue in the Sydney Pratt Memorial Room. And what we'll do in there is—(*As a great treat*) play a word game.

This is greeted with great enthusiasm by the younger members of the club, and barely suppressed groans by the older ones. They rise and cluster round the door to the Sydney Pratt Memorial Room. Charlie and one of the older girls hang back a bit from the pack. He whispers something to her. She giggles. The door to the Sydney Pratt Memorial Room opens

Mr Quigley and Davina Horrobin try to get out through the hordes of Youth Club members

Revd Elkins (*moving through the crowd*) All right. Stand back. Let Mr Quigley and the lady out, please.

The Youth Club members move back. Mr Quigley and Davina come through

Good-evening. All right, through we go, blokes and blokettes.

Revd Elkins leads the way into the Sydney Pratt Memorial Room

Mr Quigley and Davina come into the centre of the acting area

Mr Quigley (*as he passes Ed*) Oh, evening, Ed. Going to see her later, are you?

Ed (*with a grin*) Yeah.

Mr Quigley Good on you, lad.

Ed goes through into the Sydney Pratt Memorial Room

Charlie and the girl who were lingering are now moving with lascivious intent towards the DC exit

The Revd Elkins appears again in the doorway of the Sydney Pratt Memorial Room

Revd Elkins Charlie! Katie! None of that. Back here.

Reluctantly and sheepishly Charlie and the girl go back to the Sydney Pratt Memorial Room

The Revd Elkins ushers them inside and closes the door behind them

Mr Quigley So, what d'you reckon?
Davina The room's ideal.
Mr Quigley Seen a lot of children's parties, that room has.
Davina Well, it'll be fine for Candida and her friends.
Mr Quigley If you need to use the kitchen, (*He indicates* UR) it's...
Davina Won't need to. Bring everything wrapped in foil from home.
Mr Quigley Right you are.
Davina And you're sure the date's all right?
Mr Quigley (*going to his cubby-hole*) Pretty sure. I'll double-check, though.

He opens the door to his cubby-hole and goes inside

(*Off*) Pride myself on not getting the bookings mixed up, you know.

He emerges, holding his blue Village Hall bookings book

Let's have a look then. (*He consults the book*) No, that's fine. What time were you thinking?
Davina I'll invite them for five-thirty to eight—I don't think I could cope with more than two and a half hours of the little monsters. Would that be all right?
Mr Quigley Sure. Only other thing in the hall is the F.A.D.S.

Davina looks at him curiously

Local amateur dramatics. They got a Dress Rehearsal for their next show.

Davina Oh, but won't there be a lot of noise?

Mr Quigley No problem. They work in the big hall—(*he indicates off* L) through there. You won't hear a thing.

Davina Fine.

Mr Quigley (*taking a ball-point out of his overall pocket*) I'll book you in then, Mrs Horrobin. Anything else I should know about?

Davina Oh, I have booked an entertainer for the party. To take the pressure off me for half an hour or so.

Mr Quigley You doing the whole party on your own then, are you? Hubby not helping?

Davina Er, well, no. My husband is a very busy man and, er... (*She quickly changes the subject*) The entertainer's name's Professor Phun.

Mr Quigley Poor bloke. Anything else, was there?

Davina Well, one thing... The lights in that room are a bit harsh. I was wondering whether there's anything we could do to soften them down a bit...?

Mr Quigley Soften 'em down? Hm. (*He starts to have a matchmaking idea*) Tell you what—my boy Ivor might have an idea.

Davina Oh?

Mr Quigley Yeah, he's a whizz with lights and that. (*He moves* R) He's through fixing the stuff for the F.A.D.S. at the moment. Come and have a word.

Davina Fine.

Mr Quigley leads Davina off UR

The door from the Sydney Pratt Memorial Room opens to reveal Dan coming out

Noise of a rowdy guessing game is heard from inside

Dan Won't be a moment, RevJim. Just got to go to the Gents. (*He closes the door*)

The sounds of the guessing game cease. Dan, with a satisfied smile on his face, moves across UR *to where the coats and bags are. He opens one bag and pulls out a bottle of vodka. He has a swig, then crosses to the table of drinks. He selects a lemonade bottle which has only a little lemonade in the bottom and tops it up from the vodka bottle. Then he thinks for a moment. Having made his decision, he grins. He crosses back* UR, *selects a bag (different from the one he'd taken it out of) and puts the empty bottle in, so that the screw top is visible*

He crosses to the Sydney Pratt Memorial Room and goes back inside

There is a burst of guessing game noise while the door is open

> *Mr Quigley, Davina and Ivor enter from the* UL *entrance. Ivor still thinks Davina is the most beautiful creature he has ever seen*

Mr Quigley (*in the middle of a conversation*) No, Ivor's done some good effects in that room. Haven't you, Ivor?

Ivor (*mesmerised by Davina*) Sorry, Dad?

Mr Quigley I was saying you've done some good lighting effects in the Sydney Pratt, haven't you?

Ivor Oh yes, certainly, yes.

Davina What kind of things?

Ivor (*at a loss*) Er.... Well... Um... (*He looks to his father for help*)

Mr Quigley Some very clever effects. Tell you what—simplest thing, Ivor—why don't you take Mrs Horrobin out for a quick drink at the *Queen's Head* and tell 'er about them?

Ivor Well, er....

Davina I'm not sure that I've got time to——

Mr Quigley Go on, *Queen's Head's* right next door. You've got time for a drink, Mrs Horrobin.

Davina (*beginning to find Ivor rather attractive*) Well... All right, just a quick one.

Ivor stands open-mouthed, not keeping up with what's happening

Mr Quigley (*prompting*) Just a quick one, the lady said, Ivor.

Ivor Erm...

Mr Quigley (*patiently*) Mrs Horrobin has agreed to go and have a quick drink with you in the *Queen's Head* to talk about possible lighting effects in the Sydney Pratt, Ivor.

Ivor (*slowly coming to his senses*) Yes. Right. Mrs Horrobin, let's go and have a quick drink in the *Queen's Head* to talk about possible lighting effects in the Sydney Pratt.

Davina Fine.

Ivor (*very politely*) After you, Mrs Horrobin.

She smiles a thank-you and goes out through the DC exit

Ivor follows sedately behind her, then just before going out, turns back to give his father a smile of gratitude

Ivor exits

Mr Quigley shakes his head with amusement at his son's behaviour and goes across into his cubby-hole

The door to the Sydney Pratt Memorial Room opens and the Revd Elkins comes out, followed by the Youth Club members

Revd Elkins Well, what a jolly good game that was. Fun without being vulgar. Bet we could all do with a glass of pop after that, couldn't we?

The Youth Club members respond with varying degrees of enthusiasm, and cross to the table to start pouring drinks. Dan moves quickly to try and grab hold of the doctored bottle of lemonade, but Tracey gets there before him. She holds the bottle thoughtfully and picks up a beaker. Dan watches her closely during the ensuing dialogue

Charlie Have you decided when we're going to have our disco, RevJim?

Revd Elkins No, not yet. I must talk to Mr Quigley and check which Saturdays are free.

Ed Can't we do something different this year?

Revd Elkins What do you mean?

Ed Well, the disco's been exactly the same every year since I joined the Youth Club.

Charlie That's right. We even have the same records every time.

Revd Elkins Nothing wrong with that. Cliff Richard's a jolly good singer. And, coincidentally, he's a Christian. I think it's fun having the disco the same every year, don't you?

The expressions and reactions of the Youth Club members show disagreement

What do you want to make different?

Ed Well, for example, why not make it fancy dress?

Revd Elkins What kind of fancy dress?

Tracey My mum and dad went to a good fancy dress party. It was Vicars and Tarts.

Revd Elkins Yes, I don't think that's a very good idea, Tracey.

Charlie No, because we've only got one vicar.

Dan Plenty of tarts, though.

The girls remonstrate

Revd Elkins Quiet, quiet, please. I suppose a fancy dress party might be all right ... if we chose a suitable theme.

Charlie When my brother started at university, in Fresher's Week they had a toga party.

Revd Elkins A toga party?

Charlie Yes. Everyone went wrapped up in a bed sheet like Romans.

Revd Elkins With clothes on underneath, I hope.

Charlie (*with a snigger*) That was up to the individual.

Revd Elkins Hm. Well, it's an interesting idea. I'm not averse to change, you know. In many ways I'm quite "with it". So ... how many of you would like our disco this year to be a toga party?

Enthusiastic assent from all members

All right, fine. That's what we'll do. Just two conditions.

Charlie What?

Revd Elkins One—you all have to wear clothes under your togas.

The members giggle at this

And two—we'll still have music by Cliff Richard.

The members groan

I'm sure we'll have lots of fun—a jolly good, wholesome evening.

The expressions on the members' faces show how much they relish the prospect

And at the end of it I hope none of you'll forget to say thank-you to the appropriate person. Remember, it's God who made discos ... and Cliff Richard.

Tracey pours herself a beakerful from the doctored lemonade bottle and looks at the drink in her glass. Dan looks on wistfully, but she still has a firm hold on the bottle

Tracey Did God make lemonade too, RevJim?

Revd Elkins Yes, Tracey. God made everything.

Tracey In seven days, isn't that right?

Revd Elkins Yes. Well, six actually. On the seventh day He rested.

Tracey Mm. Well, you can understand. I mean, if He'd made everything in six days, He must've been knackered, mustn't He?

Revd Elkins Yes. Yes, well, I expect He was.

Tracey Which day did He make lemonade on?

Revd Elkins Er.... Well, He made the waters and the "fruit trees bearing fruit" on the third day, so the ingredients were there then. But lemonade is actually made by men and women, who weren't made until the sixth day, so I suppose you could say He really made lemonade on the sixth day.

Tracey Right. Jolly good stuff, anyway.

Revd Elkins Oh yes, jolly good.

Tracey takes a big gulp from her glass. She clutches at her throat and starts coughing

What on earth's the matter, Tracey?

Unable to speak, she points to her beaker. The Revd Elkins takes the beaker from her and sniffs it. He is furious

Stop, everyone! Quiet! Be absolutely still!

They all freeze, surprised by what's happening. The Revd Elkins takes the lemonade bottle from Tracey and sniffs it

One of you young people... One of you young people has betrayed my trust. This bottle is full of vodka.

Varying reactions from the Youth Club members—but they are all quite scared to see him so angry

I demand to know which one of you brought vodka into the hall this evening!

No response

I will find out—if I have to search the entire building, I will find out. (*He moves across to the* UR *area*) All right—all stand still. I'm going to look through the pockets of your coats—and through your bags too. (*He sees the bag with the bottle-top poking out*) Well, that wasn't very difficult, was it? (*He picks up the bag*) And not very clever on behalf of the person who did it. (*He lifts up the bag*) All right, whose is this?

Ed It's mine, but——

Revd Elkins Edward Quigley, I am disgusted at you!

Ed Look, yes, it's my bag, but——

Revd Elkins No excuses! Excuses are the coward's way out, Edward Quigley! (*He holds the bag out to Ed*) Take this! Go on, take it! Get your coat, and go!

Ed But, RevJim, I——

Revd Elkins Do not argue with me!

Reluctantly, Ed takes the bag

Get your coat!

Reluctantly, Ed goes to get his coat

And go!

Ed Look, I——

Revd Elkins (*terrifyingly angry*) Go! (*He points to the* DC *exit*) Go on!

Reluctantly, Ed moves down stage

Do as you're told! And don't think about coming back! This Youth Club can do without your sort, thank you very much!

Ed realizes his case is hopeless and hurries out of the DC *exit*

Right, the rest of you drink up your drinks and go back into the Sydney
Pratt Memorial Room. Then we'll sing some more songs—let some
nice Christian music take away the nasty taste of what's happened.

*The Youth Club members, all subdued after the outburst, drain their
drinks quickly and move back into the Sydney Pratt Memorial Room*

*Only Dan, who looks rather pleased with himself, sidles off UR and goes
out through the door to the toilets*

The Revd Elkins turns to Tracey

Are you all right, Tracey?

Tracey (*a bit tiddly*) Yes, thank you. The after-taste's quite nice, actually,
  isn't it? (*She giggles*) Which day do you think God made vodka?

Revd Elkins I don't know.

Tracey Coo, and you call yourself a vicar.

Revd Elkins Tracey...

Tracey I should think He probably made it on the sixth day—same as the
  lemonade.

Revd Elkins Probably.

Tracey (*giggling*) It'd explain why He had to rest on the seventh,
  wouldn't it? I mean, if He was hung-over...

*Revd Elkins shoves her and the last of the Youth Club members, into the
Sydney Pratt Memorial Room*

Revd Elkins Get in there, Tracey!

He follows her into the room and closes the door behind them

*Keith Horrobin, dressed in a suit and another bright tie, enters DC. As
ever, he carries his portable phone. He is crossing to Mr Quigley's
cubby-hole when the phone rings. He presses a button to make the
connection*

Keith Hallo, Keith Horrobin (*Very smarmily*) Howard, how good to hear
  you. Well, I'm at the Village Hall right now. Just got to do a small ...
  personnel rationalisation and then... Fine. If you're passing ... yes. See

you in about five minutes, Howard. (*He switches off the phone, goes straight across to Mr Quigley's cubby-hole and knocks sharply on the door*)

There is no immediate response

(*Not loudly enough for Mr Quigley to hear*) Come on, hurry up, you old fool. (*He knocks on the door again*)

Mr Quigley opens it and stands there, beaming

The sound of a television programme is heard from the room while the door is open

Mr Quigley 'Evening. What can I do you for?
Keith Something I'd like to discuss, Mr Quigley. It's committee business. May I come in?
Mr Quigley 'Course you can. In you come.

They both enter the cubby-hole and close the door behind them

The sound of the television programme is cut off

Dan enters from the UR *entrance. He goes across to the table and picks up the doctored bottle that Tracey has put down there. He takes a long swig*

Paula enters from DC

Dan sees her

Dan Paula. Good-evening. I didn't think your mother was letting you come down here any more. Too much common riff-raff, eh?
Paula I just managed to get away for a little while. Where is everyone?

Dan nods towards the Sydney Pratt

Is Ed here?
Dan No. He was here earlier ... but he left.

Paula (*disappointedly*) Oh. (*She turns towards the exit*) Was he going straight home, because I——
Dan No. He wasn't going straight home.
Paula (*turning back to face Dan; even more disappointedly*) Where'd he go then?
Dan You know Laura?
Paula What, tall Laura? The hairdresser?
Dan Yeah, the one they call "Chips".
Paula I never understood why she gets called "Chips".
Dan Oh, didn't you? It's because she goes with everything.

Paula looks shocked. Dan continues, very casually

Anyway, Ed went off with her. In her car.

Paula totters with shock. Dan comes forward and puts his arm round her for support. He pours from the lemonade bottle into an empty plastic beaker on the table. He hands it to her with his free hand

Here, have some lemonade.
Paula (*after taking a long gulp*) That's vodka.
Dan Just what you need after the shock you've had, love.

Paula starts crying

You tell me all about it.

Taking the vodka bottle, and still with an arm round Paula, he leads her UR

You have a good cry and tell your Uncle Dan all about it.

Dan and Paula exit

Keith emerges from Mr Quigley's cubby-hole

The old man is not visible

Keith Yes, I can understand you're upset at the moment, but in a week or two, you'll see the logic of it.

Lord Grevesham enters

Good-night, Mr Quigley. (*He closes the door and turns to see Lord Grevesham*) Howard. (*He goes across to shake Lord Grevesham's hand*) How good to see you.

They shake hands

Lord Grevesham And you, Keith. What brings you here?

Keith Working for our mutual benefit, actually. The superstore. Just given the old caretaker his marching orders.

Lord Grevesham Good man.

Keith Is that what you wanted to see me about?

Lord Grevesham No. It's about the other business.

Keith The parliamentary...?

Lord Grevesham nods

What about it?

Lord Grevesham Fact is, the current MP's in a spot of bother...

Keith Oh?

Lord Grevesham Sex scandal. Three-in-a-bed romps—and he was the only one of the three who wasn't a minor. The *Sun*'s leading with the story tomorrow.

Keith So what's his current situation?

Lord Grevesham He denies every word of it, and the PM says he's backing him all the way.

Keith (*understanding the implications*) So that means...

Lord Grevesham ...he'll be out by the end of the week, yes. Could mean a by-election. Best thing the local party can do is to have a really solid candidate ready to replace him.

Keith Ah.

Lord Grevesham I think you're the man, Keith. But we've got to move quickly.

Keith So will you still be coming to the house next Saturday?

Lord Grevesham No. I've met your wife and daughter—they're very photogenic—we can take them as read. What I haven't seen yet is you at work. Controlling a committee meeting.

Keith Ah.

Lord Grevesham Can you set one up?

Keith A committee meeting?

Lord Grevesham nods

Which committee? I'm on quite a few.

Lord Grevesham This one. The Village Hall lot. I'll come in as an observer. I want to see you get them to agree the superstore proposal.

Keith Oh. OK. When?

Lord Grevesham Only time I'm free in the next fortnight is the time we arranged for me to come to your house.

Keith Right. That'll be fine.

Lord Grevesham (*reaching out his hand to take Keith's*) Good man. You know, this could be the beginning of something really big for you, Keith.

Keith Thank you, Howard.

Lord Grevesham (*looking at his watch*) Must go. (*He moves to exit* DC) See you at the meeting.

Lord Grevesham exits

Keith You can rely on me. (*He looks excited, then has a thought and rushes across to Mr Quigley's cubby-hole. He opens the door without knocking*) Mr Quigley, I need you to rearrange some bookings for me.

Keith disappears inside

Dan leads Paula in from UR. *He has his arm round her and holds the empty lemonade bottle. She is weepy and a bit unsteady*

Dan Don't worry, love. I'll drive you home.

Paula But I shouldn't really...

Dan (*putting the empty lemonade bottle down on the table*) No problem. Be happy to do it.

He leads her gently down stage

I'll see you straight home, all safe and sound ... unless of course you'd like to go the pretty way...

Just before they exit, Ivor and Davina enter

Ivor looks curiously at them

Dan leads Paula out DC

Ivor 'Ere, that's Paula isn't it? What're you...?

But it's too late. They've gone. Ivor looks after them angrily

Davina And you say you've got three children, Ivor?

Ivor (*bringing himself back to Davina*) Yeah. Ed and then Kylie and Anneka. (*He chuckles*) Little terrors those two are—should see 'em doing their judo. You just got the one?

Davina Candida, yes. (*Slightly sadly*) Keith never seemed to find time for any more... (*She abruptly changes the subject*) Thank you so much for the drink, Ivor. It was so kind of you.

Ivor (*embarrassed*) Nah.

Davina It's just such a relief to talk to a man who listens.

Ivor Yeah, well, I'm sure things'll get better between you and your husband.

Davina I don't know why you take his side.

Ivor Well, you know, 'cause most people've got more good than bad in them, and I——

Keith comes hurriedly out of Mr Quigley's cubby-hole

Davina, who had been quite close to Ivor, moves away from him

Keith (*shouting at Mr Quigley inside*) Just sort it out! That's all I'm saying.

Mr Quigley emerges from his cubby-hole

Mr Quigley But——

Keith Come on—you keep boasting you've never made a double-booking in thirty years. See if you can keep that record—go out on a high note, eh? (*He turns and is surprised to see Davina*) Davina, what the hell're you doing here!

Davina I was just——

Keith (*grabbing her hand*) I'm not interested. Come on!

Davina (*indicating Ivor*) But I'd like you to meet——

Keith I am not interested in your friends—(*he looks at Ivor*) particularly
not in your rough trade.

Davina Keith——

Keith Shut it, Davina! (*He hurries her to the exit*) I've got a hell of a lot
to do!

Davina But, Keith——

Keith (*on the way out*) Shut up, you silly cow!

Keith and Davina exit

Ivor (*inarticulate with rage*) Ooh, I'd like to... With a bloke like that I'd
like to... (*He clenches his fists*) I'd like to...

Mr Quigley (*quietly furious*) So would I, Ivor. So would I. (*He looks at
his son with narrowed eyes*) And, what's more, I'm bloody going to!

*The door from the Sydney Pratt Memorial Room opens and Tracey,
clearly in desperate need, rushes across to the toilets*

*As soon as the door is opened, the sound of the Revd Elkins, who is just
visible in the doorway, and his Youth Club chorus is heard, singing
Kumbaya*

Revd Elkins   Someone singing, Lord...
All   Kumbaya.
Revd Elkins   Someone praying, Lord...

*As soon as Mr Quigley hears the singing, he strides across to the Sydney
Pratt Memorial Room door*

All   Kumbaya.
Revd Elkins   Oh, Lo-o-rd——
All   Kum——
Mr Quigley Shut up, you stupid little git! (*In fury, he slams the door shut*)

Black-out

ACT II

The calendar now reads "Saturday 19th". The committee table and chairs are laid out as at the beginning of Act I. Leaning against the back wall, either side of the hatch, are two collections of quasi-Roman banners and pikestaffs, one lot with red decorations, the other with blue. To one side of the stage is a small table with a chair in front of it. On the table is a console, with a tape recorder, speakers, headphones, tapes, script, etc., i.e. this is the place from which the production's sound effects will emanate

On stage are the Soldiers taking part in the Julius Caesar *battle scenes. They include Ed and Veronica and anyone else, male or female, whose arm Martyn has managed to twist sufficiently to get them to take part*

Their costumes are very "Coarse Acting", i.e. uneven in quality, to put it kindly. One or two are dressed in quite convincing Roman costumes, but for the others there is a lot of silver-painted dishcloth chain-mail, gold-sprayed cardboard breastplates, etc. Ed is one of the few who actually look good in a neat tunic, fitting breastplate and helmet. He has in his belt a short, painted, wooden sword. Benji also, in his role as Mark Antony, has very good armour and a helmet with a high feathered plume. Veronica, on the other hand, is wearing nothing that fits. In particular, her helmet is at least three sizes too big. It dwarfs her head and muffles her speech. Ivor is also present, sitting at the table with the tape recorder and headphones on it

As the Lights come up, Martyn Graves—with the "help" of Benji Sparrow—is instructing his armies on their movements in the battle scenes. He holds his script in its ring-file, and is coming to the end of his instructions to the Soldiers

Martyn So, luvvies, have you got that? I've spent a lot of time orchestrating these movements, but they are basically very simple. Just make sure you do the right entrances on the right cues.

Veronica (*muffled by her helmet*) Merfummerfummerfumderdlefimbum?
Martyn Sorry, Veronica, what was that?
Veronica (*still muffled*) Fimfum——

*Benji crosses and lifts her helmet off. Veronica looks rather embarrassed.
Her voice is smaller than ever*

I was just wondering how we're going to be able to hear the cues...?
Martyn Ah. Good point.

Veronica simpers at the compliment

Thanks to the wonders of modern technology and the skills of (*he
gestures to Ivor*) Ivor here ... we will have the sound of the action
relayed from the stage into here... Isn't that right, Ivor?
Ivor Yes. Won't have it switched through all the time, but I'll be able to
hear it on the headphones. Just before the cues, though, I'll switch the
tannoy on—like so. (*He throws a switch*)

Immediately, the sound of Lydia's voice is heard

*During the following, the first reaction of the assembled Soldiers is
surprise, then amusement and giggles (though not so loud that the
audience can't hear the words from the stage)*

Lydia's Voice (*very sexily*) Why don't we nip off to my dressing room
for a few minutes now, Rod?
Rod's Voice (*very embarrassed*) Well, I think I should be concentrating
on my part.
Lydia's Voice Sounds fun. Can I concentrate on it too?
Rod's Voice I mean I should concentrate on Brutus.
Lydia's Voice Spoilsport.

*As soon as he realizes what they're hearing—just after Lydia has said
"spoilsport", Martyn crosses to Ivor's table and switches the tape
recorder off*

Martyn Right, so you get the idea. Now it's simply a matter of
concentration. Make sure you know the cues, you know which side you
enter from, and—most important—you know which army you're

meant to be at any given time. Do be sure you're carrying the right banners and weapons—OK?

Veronica Erm… Do we say anything?

Martyn Good point. Thanks for mentioning it, Veronica love.

Veronica simpers again

War cries.

Ed War cries?

Martyn (*searching through his script*) Yes… Now, I did work out some war cries…

Ed We could shout—(*in football crowd style*) "Come on, you Ro-omans!"

Most of the other Soldiers think this is a good idea and start chanting "Come on, you Ro-omans!"

Martyn (*quietening them with difficulty*) Yes. Thank you, thank you, yes.

They become quiet

The only problem with that, Ed, is that this is a civil war. Both sides are Romans.

Ed Oh.

Martyn (*finding his place in the script*) Here we are. Now when you're Brutus's army, I want you all to shout, "A-Brutus! A-Brutus!"

The Soldiers don't look very keen on this. They much preferred shouting "Come on, you Ro-omans!"

Now can we just have a go at that? On a count of three. One—two—three!

Soldiers (*pretty flatly*) A-Brutus! A-Brutus!

Martyn Well, I hope when we do the run, I can rely on you to give it a bit more oomph. And, um, when you're Antony and Octavius's army, I want you to shout "Antony and Octavius—Yah!"

Benji (*dismissively*) "Antony and Octavius—Yah"?

Martyn Yes, Benji. I think that has a good Roman feel to it.

Benji Rubbish. It'll sound like a meeting of Labrador Rescue. (*Going into very Sloaney voice*) "Have you by any chance met Antony and Octavius? Yah."

Martyn No, it's not meant to be like that. It's an aggressive "Yah!" (*He tries to sound aggressive—he's not very good at it*) Yah!

Benji Well, I think they should shout, "God for Antony!" Like "God for Harry!" in *Henry V*.

Martyn What about Octavius?

Benji I don't think Octavius is very important in this part of the play— any part of the play, come to that. No, it's Antony who commands the soldiers' loyalty, after all.

Martyn (*looking confusedly into his text*) Mm...

Benji (*taking advantage*) So "God for Antony" it is then—OK?

Martyn Well...

Veronica Could I make a tiny point?

Benji What?

Veronica The Romans didn't believe in one god, did they? They believed in lots of gods. So really we should shout, "Gods for Antony!", shouldn't we?

Benji But that sounds silly.

Martyn (*seizing the initiative again*) No, I think that's a good idea. OK, luvvies, so when you're Antony and Octavius's army, you shout, "Gods for Antony and Octavius!"

Benji But——

Martyn On a count of three. One—two—three!

Soldiers (*pretty flatly and raggedly, but with a big hiss on the "s"*) Gods for Antony and Octavius!

Benji (*petulantly*) Well, if you want the show to be a laughing stock... (*He stalks* UL) Some of us are trying to give proper performances here, you know, but we keep being brought down by amateurs!

He flounces off in a huff

Martyn (*looking at his watch*) OK, we'd better move along now. Remember—most of the time you can stay in the dressing rooms or the wings. It's only for the massed entrances and exits that you need to come in here. (*He consults his script*) Now we're going to start this run at Act Four, Scene Two. "Enter Brutus, Lucilius, Lucius, *and Soldiers*"— that's you, luvvies, so you're Brutus's army first—blue banners.

Veronica (*enthusiastically*) And we shout, "A-Brutus! A-Brutus!"

Martyn No, you only do that in the battle. For heaven's sake, Veronica, we haven't got to the battle yet!

Veronica (*quashed*) Oh.

Martyn So your cue to enter will be… (*He consults the script*)
"And some that smile have in their hearts, I fear,
Millions of mischiefs."
Veronica Who says that?
Martyn Octavius.
Veronica But I thought you said Octavius's got flu.
Martyn Oh, damn, yes. So he has. All right, I'll read it in. You'll hear the cue from me. "Millions of mischiefs"—remember. And you follow Brutus on from stage left, so go through *that* door—OK? (*He points* UL *and moves towards the* DL *exit*) Right, luvvies, break a few legs.

Martyn exits L

Veronica (*bewildered*) Break a few legs?
Ed We'd better get our banners. And, Dad, you'd better switch through for the cue.
Ivor Right.

Ivor puts his headphones on and listens. The Soldiers cross to collect blue banners and pikestaffs. Veronica puts her helmet back on and walks straight into the wall. She recovers herself and manages to get the last banner, which is broken half-way down, so that its top dangles awkwardly

They've started. I'll switch it through.
Benji's Voice (*very mannered and Shakespearean, pronouncing every syllable, rather in the style of Olivier's Richard III*)
"—and our best means stretched;
And let us presently go sit in council,
How covert matters may be best disclosed,
And open perils surest answ-er-èd."
Martyn's Voice (*very limp—he's not really much of an actor—not much of a director either, come to that*) "Let us do so for we are at the stake,
And bay'd about with many enemies;
And some that smile have in their hearts, I fear,
Millions of mischiefs."
Ed That's it. (*He starts to chant*) 'Ere we go—'ere we go—'ere we go!

The other Soldiers take up the chant and scramble untidily off UL.

Veronica, totally blind in her helmet, is whirled about in the crowd and leaves the stage backwards

Ivor takes off his headphones, switches off the speaker and goes across into his father's cubby-hole

Dan and Charlie enter DC. *They are wearing knotted sheets as togas over their ordinary clothes. Dan carries a bag and looks around him to check that nobody's there*

Charlie You reckon you're going to get anywhere with that Paula Hewlett?

Dan Of course I am. I get somewhere with all the ones I fancy. And her mother approves of me like mad, because she knows my parents and I went to the right schools and everything.

Charlie Yes, but what about Paula herself?

Dan Paula'll come round. I find most women come round when they've got enough of this in them. (*He takes a bottle of vodka out of his bag*)

Charlie You're going to be in trouble if RevJim finds that.

Dan He's not going to find it.

Charlie Come on, not that many places to hide a bottle under a toga, are there?

Dan It won't be under my toga. (*He pours the contents of the vodka bottle into the glass carafe in front of Bernard's place at the committee table*) See, I'll know where it is when I want it and the empty bottle will be chucked out of the window of the Gents. (*He moves across* UR) Come on, let's go and have a quick smoke before RevJim arrives.

Charlie Right.

Charlie and Dan exit UR

Mr Quigley and Ivor come out of the cubby-hole

Mr Quigley Just a few things I got to do first, OK, Ivor. Fill up the water bottle for... (*He looks at the water carafe on the committee table*) Funny, I could've sworn I hadn't filled that... Dear oh dear, the old brain really is on the blink. Definitely time I was retiring.

Ivor Don't let Keith Horrobin hear you say that.

Mr Quigley I said "retiring". Retiring when *I* choose—not being booted out the minute some little smart-arse decides he wants to get rid of me.

Ivor (*going across to his table*) I'll just check it's switched through. You go back inside.
Mr Quigley (*moving back towards his cubby-hole*) Right you are.
Ivor And make some noise—OK?
Mr Quigley (*at the door*) What kind of noise?
Ivor Leave it to you, Dad.

Mr Quigley nods and goes back inside his cubby-hole, closing the door behind him

Ivor fiddles with his console and throws a switch

Mr Quigley's Voice (*heard over the speaker; singing tunelessly*)
            Seven in a bed and the little one said:
            "Roll over, roll over."
            And they all rolled over and one fell out
            And the little one said:
            "Roll over, roll over."
            Six in a bed and the little——

Ivor switches off the speaker and goes across to the cubby-hole door. He opens it. Mr Quigley is heard, still singing

Mr Quigley (*off*)   And they all rolled over and one fell out
                  And the little one——
Ivor Works a treat, Dad. You can stop now.

Mr Quigley comes to the door carrying his blue book

Mr Quigley Oh, good.
Ivor Wish you'd tell me what you want it for.
Mr Quigley All be clear in time, son. See you in a min. Just a couple of things to check through.

Mr Quigley closes the door

Ivor moves towards his table

The Julius Caesar *army comes rushing in* DR

Ivor hurries across to the table

Ed We've got to be Cassius's army next. Are they red?

Some of the Soldiers go to start changing banners

Veronica No, they're blue. They're on the same side as Brutus.
Ed What's the cue?
Veronica   "Hark! he is arrived.
                              March gently on to meet him."

Ivor throws a switch on his console

Rod's Voice (*from the speaker*) "Hark! he is arrived.
                              March gently on to meet him."
Ed Come on! Back the way we came!

*In some confusion, the Soldiers—once again spinning the unsighted
Veronica in their midst—rush back through the DR exit*

Ivor switches off the speaker

*Davina and Candida enter DC. Both are wearing their Barbours again.
Davina pushes a serving trolley, piled high with trays, on which are
silver-foil-wrapped packages. Candida carries a pile of trays. On the
top of Davina's pile is a tray of individual jellies, and on the top of
Candida's a tray of individual custard trifles. Davina also has a
shopping bag hanging from her arm*

Ivor turns to see them

Ivor 'Ere. Let me give you a hand with some of that.
Davina Oh, bless you, Ivor. Candida, this is the nice man I told you about.
   Ivor Quigley—my daughter Candida.

Ivor helps to extricate the shopping bag from Davina's arm

Ivor Pleased to meet you.
Candida And I'm pleased to meet you. Living the sort of life I lead, and

going to the sort of school I do, I don't often get a chance to meet common people.

Davina (*shocked*) Candida!

Ivor (*with a grin*) Don't worry about it. Being the sort of bloke I am, and doing the sort of work I do, I don't often get the chance to meet toffee-nosed little prigs. (*He holds his hand out to Candida*)

There is a moment's pause, while she considers how to react. Then she giggles and holds out her hand to his. They shake

You go into the room and we can pass the stuff through the hatch.

Davina gives Ivor the trolley

Davina (*going to the door of the Sydney Pratt Memorial Room*) Fine.

She goes into the room

Ivor pushes the trolley up to in front of the hatch

Ivor (*managing to extricate an aerosol from the shopping basket*) What're these for? All going to start shaving, are you?

Candida No, you twit. It's whipped cream—for the jellies.

Ivor Oh. My two little ones'd like this stuff.

Candida What're they called, your little ones?

Ivor Kylie and Anneka.

Candida Oh, gosh. It must be thrilling to have a common name, mustn't it?

Ivor looks at her rather dubiously

No, I mean it. I'm sick to death of being boring old Candida. I'd much rather be ... (*she gets increasingly carried away by the beauty of the ensuing names*) Charlene ... or Rayette ... or ... (*life can hold no more for her*) Sharon...

Ivor Well, I'm going to call you Candy.

Candida Candy? Oh, I like that. It's almost common.

Ivor gives her an amused look

The hatch doors to the Sydney Pratt Memorial Room open to reveal Davina framed in them

The lighting behind her is a lot more subtle than it was in Act I and there are a few balloons etc. in evidence

Davina This is brilliant, Ivor. The lighting—you've really made it look wonderful.
Ivor (*embarrassed*) Nah. Wasn't nothing to it.

He starts passing trays through to Davina

The Soldiers come through from UL *in their usual confusion*

Davina Who on earth're these?
Ivor It's the *Julius Caesar* lot.
Davina Oh, right. Your father mentioned them.
Ed (*to Veronica*) When are we on next?
Veronica (*crossing to Ivor's table to look at his script, and having to raise her helmet to read it*) Well, Brutus and Cassius've just gone into Brutus's tent ... (*She turns the pages*) and our next cue's Act Five, Scene One—"Enter Octavius, Antony and their army".
Ed So it's red banners next, everybody ... but it's not for twenty minutes, so we can go and watch the rehearsal from out front.

The Soldiers start to change their blue banners for red ones

Jack, one of the younger Soldiers, and Veronica, get theirs early and move forward. Jack thinks Veronica knows everything about the theatre; he is a little in awe of her

During the following dialogue, the other Soldiers, except Ed, trickle out through the upstage and DR *exits*

Jack Erm, Veronica ... what do you think's the best way to hold these banners?
Veronica (*airily*) Oh, just hold them as if you were carrying a bit of Birnan Wood in The Scottish Play.
Jack What's The Scottish Play?

Veronica (*patiently*) A certain play by one W Shakespeare about a thane who kills the king and takes over the throne.

Jack Oh, you mean *Macb*——

Veronica leaps on him and puts her hand over his mouth

Veronica Jack, don't ever do that again! Not in any theatre I'm working in—please!

She removes her hand

Jack But what did I do?

Veronica In the theatre, mentioning the name of The Scottish Play brings unbelievably bad luck.

Jack Oh. I won't do it again, don't worry. (*Admiringly*) Where do you learn all these things, Veronica?

Veronica Quite honestly, Jack luvvy, when you've been in the business as long as I have, you just *know* instinctively.

She goes off rather grandly DR

Jack (*reverently following her*) Ah. Right.

Jack exits

By now all the other Soldiers have changed their banners and trickled out through the upstage and DR *exits. Ed sees Ivor passing trays through the hatch and moves across to him*

Ed You haven't seen Paula around this afternoon, have you, by any chance, Dad?

Ivor Sorry, son.

Ed looks gloomy

Oh, Ed, like you to meet someone. My son Edward—Davina Horrobin.

Candida waves through the hatch

And Candida Horrobin.

Candida (*disappointed*) Edward? That's not a very common name. Not really at all lower class, is it? I mean, we've even got a Prince Edward.

Davina Candida, shut up. Ivor, do you think you could just help us put some of this stuff out...?

Ivor Well, by rights I should be doing the sound for... Yeah, love to, Davina.

He hurries through into the Sydney Pratt Memorial Room, closing the door behind him

At the same time Davina closes the hatch doors

Ed is left alone on stage, looking a bit wistful

Then he wanders off through the DR *exit*

The moment he is out of sight, Paula enters DC, *carrying her sports bag. She looks hopefully around, but is disappointed to find the room is empty*

Georgina (*off; calling*) Paula!

Paula (*wearily*) It's all right, Mummy. I'm here.

Georgina enters DC, *also carrying a sports bag*

Georgina I daren't let you out of my sight for a moment. I thought I could trust you, Paula, but after you went directly against my wishes the other week and came here to the Youth Club to see that oik Edward Quigley...

Paula I didn't see him, Mummy. I told you.

Georgina I can tell when you're lying, Paula.

Paula But I——

Georgina Why you can't choose a nice boy like that Daniel Carstairs, I will never know. He's at public school and his father's a stockbroker.

Paula But I don't like him.

Georgina Oh, really, Paula, stop being so pathetic! It's not a matter of "liking", it's a matter of what's appropriate. If people allowed the fact that they didn't *like* each other to stop them getting married ... well, you wouldn't be here for a start.

Paula Mummy...

Tina, Patti and Kelly come in DC, *with other members of the aerobics club*

From the moment they enter, Patti and Kelly gossip. They continue over Tina's lines and until they all go through to the changing rooms UR. *They use as much of the ensuing dialogue as there is time for*

Tina (*seeing the committee table and chairs*) Oh, really! The place hasn't even been cleared for us. It's bad enough having to change our regular day, but... I'll speak to Mr Quigley after we've all got changed.

Patti Anyway, then, Janet decides she's going to have one of her efficiency blitzes. She gets like that sometimes, as you know.

Kelly Don't I just? What was it this time—checking on the number of photocopies made?

Patti No. She'll get round to that again soon, I'm sure. No, this time it was double-spacing of faxes.

Kelly Oh yes?

Patti All faxes from now on—according to madam—have to be single-spaced, so that we cut down the total number of pages sent. Not only that...

Kelly You mean there's more?

Patti Oh yes. Letters should be reduced to half size on the photocopier so that you send even less pages.

Kelly Whatever next?

Patti Exactly. Well, you can imagine what happens first time I hand Roger a single-spaced letter to sign...

Kelly And how? "Don't they teach you anything at secretarial college these days?"

Patti Oh yes. And more of the same.

Tina and Patti follow the rest of the aerobics group who have passed through the UR *doors*

The door to the Sydney Pratt Memorial Room opens and Candida comes rushing out. She has now taken off her Barbour and is dressed in a pretty little party dress (and probably white tights and patent leather shoes)

Candida It's all right, Mummy. I saw Chloe's mummy parking the car. I'll welcome her.

Chloe comes in DC. She is the same age as Candida and talks with the same accent. She is wearing a Barbour over a pretty little party dress (and probably white tights and patent leather shoes). She holds a gift-wrapped present

Chloe (*calling back*) See you at eight, Mummy. (*She scampers forward to greet Candida*) Happy birthday, Candida. (*She kisses the air on either side of Candida's face*) Mwah. Mwah. Here's your present.

Jessica comes in DC. She is the same age as Candida and talks with the same accent. She wears a Barbour over a pretty little party dress (and probably white tights and patent leather shoes). She holds a gift-wrapped present

Davina comes out of the room and stands in a welcoming pose beside the door

Candida (*taking the present*) Thank you, Chloe.

Ivor, bemused by what's going on, stands in the doorway of the Sydney Pratt Memorial Room

He keeps trying to get out, but is constantly prevented by the arrival of a new guest

Davina Hallo, Chloe darling, do come through.

She ushers Chloe into the Sydney Pratt Memorial Room

Chloe disappears inside

Jessica (*calling back*) See you at eight, Mummy. (*She scampers forward to greet Candida*) Happy birthday, Candida (*She kisses the air on either side of Candida's face*) Mwah. Mwah. Here's your present.

Antonia comes in DC. She is the same age as Candida and talks with the same accent. She is wearing a Barbour over a pretty little party dress (and probably white tights and patent leather shoes). She holds a gift-wrapped present

Candida (*taking the present*) Thank you, Jessica.
Davina Hallo, Jessica darling, do come through.

She ushers Jessica into the Sydney Pratt Memorial Room

Jessica disappears inside

Antonia (*calling back*) See you at eight, Mummy. (*She scampers forward to greet Candida*) Happy birthday, Candida. (*She kisses the air on either side of Candida's face*) Mwah. Mwah. Here's your present.

Beatrice comes in DC. She is the same age as Candida and talks with the same accent. She is wearing a Barbour over a pretty little party dress (and probably white tights and patent leather shoes). She holds a gift-wrapped present

Candida (*taking the present*) Thank you, Antonia.
Davina Hallo, Antonia darling, do come through.

She ushers Antonia into the Sydney Pratt Memorial Room

Antonia disappears inside

Beatrice (*calling back*) See you at eight, Mummy. (*She scampers forward to greet Candida*) Happy birthday, Candida (*She kisses the air on either side of Candida's face*) Mwah. Mwah. Here's your present.

Araminta comes in DC. She is the same age as Candida and talks with the same accent. She is wearing a Barbour over a pretty little party dress (and probably white tights and patent leather shoes). She holds a gift-wrapped present

Candida Thank you, Beatrice.
Davina Hallo, Beatrice darling, do come through.

She ushers Beatrice into the Sydney Pratt Memorial Room

Beatrice disappears inside

Araminta (*calling back*) See you at eight, Mummy. (*She scampers* *forward to greet Candida)* Happy birthday, Candida. (*She kisses the air on either side of Candida's face)* Mwah. Mwah. Here's your present.

Perpetua comes in DC. She is the same age as Candida and talks with the same accent. She is wearing a Barbour over a pretty little party dress (and probably white tights and patent leather shoes). She holds a gift-wrapped present

Candida Thank you, Araminta.
Davina Hallo, Araminta darling, do come through.

She ushers Araminta into the Sydney Pratt Memorial Room

  Araminta disappears inside

Perpetua (*calling back*) See you at eight, Mummy. (*She scampers forward to greet Candida)* Happy birthday, Candida. (*She kisses the air on either side of Candida's face)* Mwah. Mwah. Here's your present.
Candida Thank you, Perpetua.
Davina Hallo, Perpetua darling, do come through.

She ushers Perpetua into the Sydney Pratt Memorial Room

  Perpetua disappears inside

(NB: the idea of this sequence is that it should accelerate with the arrival of each of the party guests. How it's played depends on how many little girls are used. If it gets too slow, they can come in in pairs after the first two)

By the end Candida is loaded down with presents

Davina Better come through and be a hostess, darling.
Candida (*going through into the Sydney Pratt Memorial Room*) Yes, Mummy.

  Candida goes into the Sydney Pratt Memorial Room

Ivor finally manages to get out of the Sydney Pratt Memorial Room. He stands, looking rather soppily at Davina. He is absolutely gone on her

Davina (*taking a deep breath*) Wish me luck.

Ivor They all seemed dead well-behaved to me.

Davina Give them ten minutes. (*She looks at her watch*) The entertainer should be here by now.

Ivor I'll send him through when he comes.

Davina His name's Professor Phun.

Ivor Poor bloke. (*Still mesmerised by Davina, he backs away from her and walks into the committee table*)

Davina See you.

Davina goes through into the Sydney Pratt Memorial Room, blowing Ivor a kiss as she goes

Ivor is sheepishly delighted at this and almost floats across to his table, where he sits down and, with a stupidly blissful expression on his face, puts on his headphones

Mr Quigley comes out of the cubby-hole, leaving the door ajar

Mr Quigley (*going across to Ivor*) Just seen some of the Village Hall Committee lot arriving in the car park.

Ivor does not react. Mr Quigley waves a hand in front of his son's face. Ivor jumps, turns and takes his headphones off

Committee lot arriving.

Ivor Anything I should be doing?

Mr Quigley No. You stay there till I tell you. I'm just going to get Mrs Millington to come through.

Mr Quigley exits DR

Ivor puts his headphones back on

Keith Horrobin enters DC. He is more smartly dressed than ever and, of course, carries his portable phone. He looks around the room, and is annoyed to see the Julius Caesar *banners and Ivor at his table*

Keith What the hell are you doing here?

Ivor does not react. Keith moves across to just behind him

I *said*, "What the hell are you doing here?"

Lydia comes in through the DL *entrance, wearing the "Grecian-style" dress she described in Act I*

(*Shouting*) What the hell are you doing here!

Ivor still does not react. Lydia replies to Keith's question

Lydia I came to see you.
Keith (*taken aback*) Ah. Lydia.
Lydia Yes, Keith. And let me tell you, a pretty angry Lydia.
Keith Why should you be angry?
Lydia Because I discovered inadvertently from Bernard this morning that
   you'd called a Special Meeting of the Village Hall Committee for this
   evening, and I hadn't been told about it.
Keith Ah yes. Well, it was because of this. (*He indicates her dress*) I
   mean, I knew you'd got a Dress Rehearsal and wouldn't be able to come,
   so I didn't bother you by mentioning it.
Lydia Huh.
Keith (*trying to hustle her off* DL) And shouldn't you be getting back to
   your Dress Rehearsal? I mean, they can't do *Julius Caesar* without
   Portia, can they?

At this moment Ivor unplugs his headphones and stretches

Rod's Voice (*over the speaker, very dramatically and emotionally*) "No
   man bears sorrow better: Portia is dead."

*Ivor, unaware that there is anyone else in the room with him, leans
forward and plugs his headphones in again, cutting off the sound from the
stage*

Lydia See. I'm dead. I'm not needed now till the curtain call, so that gives
   you plenty of time to explain why I wasn't told about the Special
   Committee Meeting.
Keith Well, it was——

Lydia It wasn't by any chance because this is the meeting where you were going to discuss the future of the Village Hall site, and you didn't want a member of the local Planning Committee there at this juncture?

Keith I can assure you that wasn't the reason.

Lydia No? And I suppose the reason that you came on to me in the first place hadn't anything to do with the fact that I was on the local Planning Committee?

Keith Lydia, that's nonsense. I "came on to you", as you put it, because I thought you were incredibly attractive.

Lydia "Thought"?

Keith Think. Think. Think you're incredibly attractive.

Lydia If I find you were just taking advantage of me, I'll see to it your life's not worth living. I'll tell everyone about our affair.

Keith Don't be ridiculous.

Lydia I don't trust you an inch, Keith Horrobin.

Keith How can you say that?

Lydia (*getting furious*) I can say it because I think you're a low, conniving rat, and if you imagine for one moment that I was ever even mildly attracted to you, then you can——

Keith shuts her up by kissing her. The tension drains out of Lydia's body, and when they draw apart, she is all avid compliance

Oh... Keith.... (*She draws close to him again*) Keith, isn't there somewhere we can go?

Keith Well, um, it's hardly the moment for...

He hears the sounds of voices coming in from DC, thinks quickly and drags the willing Lydia up towards Mr Quigley's cubby-hole. He takes a quick look inside

Go in there. I'll join you when I've——

He tries to move away, but Lydia has him by the hand and yanks him into the room, just as she did with Rod at the end of Scene 3. She kicks the door closed behind them

Bernard, Joan and the Revd Elkins enter DC. They go across to hang up their coats UR

Bernard I must say it's very inconvenient, a Special Meeting. It throws everything out. I had to start on a whole new packet of coloured stickers.

Revd Elkins And I had to cancel the Youth Club's toga party. Mr Quigley was going to ring round the members to stop them coming. I hope he's got to them all.

Joan Yes, it is a bit inconvenient. And I'm not quite sure about the correct way of doing the minutes for a Special Meeting. I mean, are they just like for an ordinary meeting or are they somehow special? Do committee members still have to speak through the chair, for example?

Bernard crosses to his chair and fills his glass from the carafe

Bernard Oh yes, committee members always have to speak through the chair. (*He takes a swig from his glass*) Hm. This water tastes decidedly odd. I wonder where on earth Mr Quigley got it from. Oh, well, I can ask him, can't I?

As the Revd Elkins and Joan take their seats, Bernard crosses to knock on the cubby-hole door

Mr Quigley. Mr Quigley!

The door opens a little and Keith sidles out, tucking his tie in and smoothing down his hair

Keith Bernard. Good-afternoon.

Bernard Is Mr Quigley in there? Because I wanted to...

Keith (*leading Bernard back to the table*) No, no, he's not in there. No-one's in there. I was just in there looking for him, and there's no-one there. No-one at all. In there. No-one.

Bernard Oh. (*He picks up his glass*) Because there's something decidedly odd about this water. (*He takes a swig*) Decidedly odd. (*He takes another swig to be sure*)

Joan Are we about to start the meeting, Mr Horrobin?

Keith No, no, not straight away. (*He flounders*) Because it concerns the, er, um... (*He has a brainwave*) Because it concerns the use of the Village Hall as a cultural venue——

He starts shepherding them off DL

—it's very important that all the committee members see a bit of the current rehearsal of *Julius Caesar*, so that they're able to speak with authority on the subject.

Revd Elkins Speak with authority on the subject?

Keith Exactly.

He pushes the bewildered trio off DL *and turns back into the room*

He looks at his watch, purses his lips, thinks for a moment, then hurries across to the cubby-hole. He opens the door and speaks very smoothly

Sorry to have kept you, my angel.

He goes in and closes the door

It is heard to be locked

Professor Phun enters, DC. *He is a lugubrious middle-aged man, wearing an overcoat over a kind of clown's outfit with a long tailcoat. He also wears a shapeless tweed hat. He carries a unicycle and a big bulging bag with a rather faded "Professor Phun" painted on the side. He sees Ivor as he comes into the room*

Professor Phun (*to Ivor*) Good-evening.

Ivor does not hear him, but this does not worry Professor Phun, who still goes into a doleful monologue as he gets ready for his act. His speech continues through his actions

Though I'd like to know just exactly what's good about it. (*He puts his bag down on the committee table and leans his unicycle against a chair. He removes his coat, opens the bag and puts the coat inside*) Bloody awful evening, if you want my opinion. Which you probably don't. (*He gets a mirror out of the bag, props it up and checks his make-up in it*) Sort of evening when anyone with half a brain should be sitting in front of the television with a few beers, not coming out to some draughty Village Hall to entertain a bunch of spoilt brats. (*He takes his cap off, takes out of the bag a tall hat with a dangly flower on top, and puts it on*) God, I hate kids. And from the sound of the mum on the phone, this is going to be an upper-class lot. They're the worst. Nothing more terrifying for an entertainer than a room full of nicely-brought-up kids. (*He takes a hooter with a bulb out of the bag and gives it an exploratory honk. Then he stows it in a pocket of his tailcoat. He slightly opens the front of his shirt and looks inside*) You all right in there, Deirdre? (*He explains to the oblivious Ivor*) My dove, Deirdre. Use her for the climax of the act. Out she comes flapping like mad—(*dispiritedly*) what a surprise. Called her Deirdre after a woman I once knew… (*He sighs*) It didn't work out. (*He starts hiding away playing cards, silk scarves, coloured balls, gold rings, etc. in various pockets of his tailcoat*) Nothing much worked out in my life, really. You know what I wanted to do when I was a nipper? Work in a bank, that was my ambition. Work as a cashier behind the glass—all I wanted to do. That didn't work out either. (*He takes some clubs out of his bag and starts practising juggling with them*) Trouble with today's nippers, you know, trouble with them is they think they know it all. What's even worse, when it comes to conjuring tricks, they do know it all. Seen them on telly, haven't they? (*He puts the clubs back in his bag and gets on to the unicycle*) Always have a quick practice before I do a booking. (*He starts cycling round the committee table, still talking*) No, as I was saying, kids nowadays've seen all the tricks on the box. They video them and slow it down so's they can see how they're done. Takes the fun out of things, doesn't it? I wonder what they do get fun from, kids these days? Not that I had much fun when I was a kid. Bloody miserable I was most of the time. My parents were bloody miserable, and all. Do you know——

Davina comes out of the Sydney Pratt Memorial Room

There is a burst of animated girlish shouting from inside when she opens the door. It cuts off the moment she closes it

Davina Oh, you must be Professor Phun.

Professor Phun (*still pedalling round on his unicycle*) Yes. I must be, mustn't I?

Davina I was starting to get worried about you.

Professor Phun Don't you ever worry about me. I'm never late. What time to do you want me to go on?

Davina Straight away, please. It'll give me half an hour to get their tea ready.

Professor Phun Half an hour? I thought we agreed on the phone it'd only be twenty minutes.

Davina Well, I was thinking … with laughs and audience reaction.

Professor Phun (*gloomily getting off his unicycle*) With laughs and audience reaction be nearer fifteen.

Davina Well, whatever. If you could start as soon as possible.

Professor Phun Yes, yes, of course. (*Lugubriously*) Another opening, another show. (*He looks down inside his shirt*) Good luck, Deirdre. (*He picks up his bag from the table*) The condemned man ate a hearty breakfast. (*He turns to Davina*) Right, show me the place of execution. (*To Ivor*) Thanks for listening, mate.

Ivor is still oblivious to everything that's been going on

Davina opens the door to the Sydney Pratt Memorial Room. There is an even louder sound of girlish shouting. Professor Phun, carrying his bag and unicycle, moves with doom-laden footsteps towards the door

Beatrice (*off; loudly, above the sound of the other little girls*) Oh, no! Not him again!

Professor Phun and Davina go through into the Sydney Pratt Memorial Room

The second the door closes behind them, the sounds from the girls inside stop

Georgina and Paula enter from UR. They are now dressed in their leotards

Georgina Paula, why weren't you more polite to Daniel when you saw him coming out of the changing room?

Paula I've told you. Because I don't like him.

Georgina Oh, for heaven's sake, girl! Why on earth not?

Paula Because he keeps putting his arm round me and trying to kiss me.

Georgina But that's what men do. It may not be very pleasant, but it's our duty as women just to put up with it.

Paula But, Mummy——

Tina, in her leotard, bustles in from UR

Tina Oh dear, that table still hasn't been moved. I must speak to Mr Quigley. (*She goes across to Mr Quigley's cubby-hole and knocks on the door*)

There is no response

As Tina is doing this, other leotarded members of the aerobics group come in from UR

Patti and Kelly enter, gossiping as ever. Their ensuing dialogue is meant to be continuous until their next exit, so they just go on, oblivious to any action around them

Patti That Nicola's no better than she should be, either. Do you remember that party of Darren's?

Kelly The one where Katie was sick all over his cat?

Patti That's right. Well, you know Darren told everyone to throw their coats over his bed?

Kelly Mm.

Patti Nobody realised that Nicola was already in the bed.

Kelly What—on her own?

Patti By no means. Give you three guesses who she was with...

Kelly Dave?

Patti You gotta be joking.

Kelly Lennie?

Patti She should be so lucky.

Kelly Patti, surely it wasn't Paul...?

Patti No, of course it wasn't Paul. It was only Roger.

Kelly Roger? Roger from the office?

Patti None other.

Kelly But who on earth did you hear it from?

Patti Well, you know Paul's friend Derek...?

Kelly In Accounts?

Patti That's the one. Well, his sister Philippa's got a boyfriend called Bill... I say "boyfriend", but I'm not actually sure how serious they are. I think he could be more of a "friend boy" than your actual "boyfriend", but, anyway ... this Bill's got a mate called Nigel, who was at Darren's party and he swears blind that his was the last coat and when he picked it up, Nicola and Roger were underneath it.

Kelly Well, there's a turn-up.

Patti That's what I thought. I mean, I don't know what men see in Nicola.

Kelly The fact that she's available.

Patti Yes, that is true. That is certainly true.

Kelly Men don't usually. But I can't imagine any of them'd want to be seen out with her. I mean, her dress sense... You'd've thought someone with hair like that'd know that, as a colour, terracotta was a bad idea.

Patti Unless she was wearing it as a joke. But I don't think she's the sort to see the funny side.

Kelly No, not highly blessed with sense of humour, is she?

Patti Thick is the word I'd use. Dead thick.

Kelly You have a point there, Kelly.

Action of the other characters after Patti and Kelly's entrance:

Tina knocks again at Mr Quigley's cubby-hole door. Getting no response, she crosses to the DL *exit*

Tina I'll see if Mr Quigley's through in the big hall. Oh, look, you lot, start the warm-up. Come on, get marching round the table! With shoulder gyrations!

The other members of the aerobic class start marching. Patti and Kelly continue chatting

All of you!

With bad grace, Patti and Kelly join the others marching round the committee table

Tina goes off DL

Patti and Kelly's conversation continues uninterrupted

The Soldiers, carrying red banners, come rushing in from the UL *entrance. Some of them get infiltrated into the aerobics circle. Somehow caught up in the midst of the Soldiers is Bernard Millington. He spins out of the crowd in some bewilderment, and makes his way through a gap in the marching aerobics group to sit in his chair. He pours himself some more from the carafe and starts sipping it*

Ed What's the next cue?

Veronica It's a very quick one. (*She goes to look over Ivor's shoulder at his script*)

Ivor becomes aware of her

"I do not cross you; but I will do so." And this time we're Brutus's army.

Ed Brutus's army! Change banners, everyone!

The Soldiers start changing their red banners for blue ones

Dad, can we have the sound up?

Ivor throws a switch on his console. Sounds from the stage join the general confusion of Patti and Kelly's conversation etc.

Benji's Voice   "...lead your battles softly on,
                               Upon the left hand of the even field."

Ed suddenly sees Paula in the aerobics group. He moves slowly towards her

Martyn's Voice   "Upon the right hand I. Keep thou the left."
Benji's Voice   "Why do you cross me in this exigent?"

Paula suddenly becomes aware of Ed. She moves out of the marching circle and moves slowly towards him

Martyn's Voice   "I do not cross you; but I will do so."

Just before Ed and Paula meet, Veronica shouts her line and grabs hold of Ed

Veronica That's the cue!

Veronica drags Ed off with the rest of the Soldiers, who go rushing through the DL *exit*

Mr Quigley comes in UL, *being torn off a strip by Tina*

Tina Well, it's very inefficient of you, Mr Quigley, to have got us double-booked.

Mr Quigley I'll sort it out in a minute, don't worry. For the time being, though, there's room for you to do a few of your exercises in the changing rooms.

Tina That's hardly the same.

Mr Quigley (*pleading*) Just while I get it sorted. (*He moves to Ivor's table*)

Tina Oh, very well. But it's extremely annoying. (*She claps her hands*) Ladies! We'll continue in the changing room—just briefly while Mr Quigley gets this place tidied up.

The aerobics group go off UR

Patti and Kelly's conversation continues until cut off by the door closing behind them. Paula tries to linger on stage

Georgina Come along, Paula!

Reluctantly, Paula follows her mother off stage

Davina, looking harassed, comes out of the Sydney Pratt Memorial Room

More raucous sounds of the little girl's party are heard for the time that the door is open

Mr Quigley How's it going then, Mrs Horrobin?

Davina Pure hell on earth. (*She wipes her brow*) At least I've got a break now while the entertainer does his stuff.

Mr Quigley taps Ivor on the shoulder and winks at him

Ivor Now?

Davina begins to move towards the UR exit

Mr Quigley nods. Ivor throws a switch. Immediately Keith and Lydia's voices are heard from the speaker. Davina freezes when she recognises her husband's voice. Bernard, who has been sitting quietly sipping vodka, also reacts when he hears Lydia's voice

Keith's Voice Of course you mean a lot to me, Lydia.

Lydia's Voice You're just saying that, Keith. You only went to bed with me because you wanted me to use my influence on the Planning Committee.

Keith's Voice Don't be ridiculous. I went to bed with you because you're a very attractive woman.

Lydia's Voice (*purring*) Hmm... Kiss me.

The sound of a kiss

But why are you so concerned to keep our affair a secret? You've told me you don't love Davina...

Keith's Voice No, I don't.

Lydia's Voice And Bernard never notices what I do, anyway. Or if he notices, he doesn't care, so he doesn't matter.

Bernard rises to his feet and is surprised to find himself somewhat unsteady

Why can't we be together all the time like proper lovers?

Keith's Voice No, we must wait, Lydia. Things're a bit tricky at the moment. Now listen, I must——

The sounds from the speaker are interrupted by the sudden banging open of the doors to the hatch from the Sydney Pratt Memorial Room

Professor Phun is framed in them, the picture of misery, covered with jelly and cream and with all the little girls behind hitting him and hurling things at him

Professor Phun Help! The little monsters're murdering me!

Professor Phun is pulled back inside the room by the little girls and the hatch doors are slammed shut on him

The girls' shouting is silenced

Davina Oh, my God, they will kill him!

She rushes off into the Sydney Pratt Memorial Room to save the entertainer

Once again there is a burst of shouting while the door is open

Bernard, still looking confused, totters back down on to his seat and pours himself another drink from the carafe

From UL *the Soldiers come rushing in. They are all brandishing swords and other weapons. Ed looks hopefully round the room and is upset that there's no sign of Paula*

Mr Quigley stands by the door of his cubby-hole, watching the mounting chaos with glee

Soldiers (*in ragged unison*) Gods for Antony and Octavius! Gods for Antony and Octavius!
Veronica We're Brutus's army next. Stay with these banners!
Ed What's the next cue?
Veronica The next entrance is "Alarum. Enter fighting soldiers of both armies."
Ivor "Alarum"?

He presses a switch. A fanfare is heard

Professor Phun comes running out of the Sydney Pratt Memorial Room. He is now trouserless and covered with jelly and cream. He clutches his bag and unicycle, and is pursued by Candida and her friends. They still look immaculate in their party dresses, but are shouting and screaming like revenging Valkyries. Davina brings up the rear, carrying Professor Phun's trousers and trying—without success—to impose some calm

Davina Look, please! Please behave yourselves, girls! Put him down!

Professor Phun tries to hide from the girls behind the Soldiers, some of whom are still changing their banners. Davina is still trying vainly to control the little horrors. Professor Phun manages to get a line of Soldiers between him and his pursuers

But then, with cries of "A-Brutus! A-Brutus!", waving their swords and blue banners, the Soldiers all rush off DL, *leaving Professor Phun once again isolated*

He reaches inside his shirt and pulls out a dangling, dead dove

Professor Phun Deirdre.

But he has no time to mourn. The little girls are advancing on him once again. He uses his unicycle as a lion tamer might a chair to fend of his attackers and works his way round to near the table. Bernard looks up at him with some confusion

Bernard (*by now quite drunk*) I say. Are you the man who's been sleeping with my wife?
Professor Phun No, of course I'm not! (*He manages to get on to his unicycle and starts cycling round the table*)

Candida and her friends pursue him. Davina still tries to stop them. She manages to grab Candida and two others and with great difficulty to hold them

Davina (*handing Professor Phun his trousers*) Quick! While the going's good!
Professor Phun Thank you! Goodbye!

He makes his escape on the unicycle DC

Davina Now you're very naughty little girls! You all go straight back into the room—and behave yourselves!

Ivor takes off his headphones and moves sympathetically towards Davina

Subdued, Candida and her friends troop meekly back into the Sydney Pratt Memorial Room

During the following, Bernard falls asleep at the committee table, lying back in his chair with his head back and mouth open

Ivor You going to be all right with them?
Davina Yes, I'm sure the worst's over now.
Ivor Don't you believe it.
Davina What do you mean?

Ivor Well, I find with my Kylie and Anneka, they get even more dreadful
    … once they've tasted blood.
Davina (*going to the door of the Sydney Pratt Memorial Room*) I'll cope.
Ivor Give us a shout if you need any help.
Davina (*blowing him another kiss*) Sure.

She disappears into the room

Ivor beams stupidly, then turns to Mr Quigley

Ivor (*to his father*) Anything else we should be doing, Dad?
Mr Quigley (*moving down stage and rubbing his hands together
    gleefully*) No, it's all wound up. Now we just have to let it run. (*He stops
    by the* DC *exit and hides in the shadows*) And I think I'll watch the next
    bit from down here. Nice grandstand view.
Ivor Right.

Ivor goes back to his sound effects table

Georgina enters UR, *ushering in Dan, still dressed in his sheet toga, and
a very reluctant Paula*

Paula But I should be doing the aerobics. Tina'll——
Georgina You can catch up on the aerobics any time. I'm sure you'll
    enjoy yourself much more having a chat with Daniel.
Paula I don't——
Dan (*very smoothly*) And then maybe, after the toga party, I could take
    Paula out for a drink…? If that would be all right with you, Mrs
    Hewlett…?
Georgina Of course, Daniel.
Dan Needless to say, I'll see to it that I bring her home at a reasonable
    hour.
Georgina Oh, don't you worry about that, Daniel. I trust you completely
    with her.
Dan (*even more smoothly*) Good.
Georgina Now I must get back to the class and try to undo some of the
    ravages of time.
Dan (*smoother than ever*) I can't see any ravages, Mrs Hewlett. Looking
    very good. You and Paula could be mistaken for sisters, you know.

Georgina (*simpering*) Oh, Daniel ... what nonsense. (*She gives a little giggle, then moves to go off*) Do give my regards to your parents, won't you?

Dan Of course, Mrs Hewlett.

Georgina goes off UL

Dan turns triumphantly to Paula

So here we are again.

Paula (*sullenly*) Yes.

Dan Just the two of us. (*He moves to the table, where Bernard still sleeps*) Have a nice little drink, shall we? (*He lifts up the carafe, surprised to see how empty it is, and pours some into a glass*) Thirsty?

Paula shakes her head

It's only water.

Paula Last time you said it was only lemonade.

Dan shrugs, takes a big swig from the glass, and puts it down on the table. He crosses purposefully to Paula and puts his arms round her. She struggles, but can't escape

Dan So, here we are together—with just a sheet between us. My idea of heaven.

Suddenly, holding her tight with his left arm, he grasps her face in his left hand and pulls her towards him for a kiss

At this moment, the Soldiers come rushing in UL. *They are waving their swords and shouting "A-Brutus! A-Brutus!" In the forefront of them is Ed. As soon as he enters, he sees Dan and Paula*

Ed Leave her alone, you bastard!

Dan and Paula spring apart. Paula runs to behind Ed. He grabs another sword from one of the other Soldiers and chucks it towards Dan

All right, let's fight for her.

Paula You don't need to fight for me. You're the only one I've ever wanted, Ed. It's you that I love.

Ed (*amazed and frozen by this news*) Really?

Slowly, Ed turns to face Paula. Slowly, they move towards each other. Dan picks up the sword. Before Paula and Ed meet, Dan rushes up behind Ed and hits him in the back

Ow! All right, if that's the way you want to play it…

They circle each other with swords and then go into a fight

Dan I'm going to win. I'm bigger and stronger than you, Ed. You're going to get a beating you certainly won't forget in a hurry.

Ed Oh yes?

They go into a wooden-sword fight, cheered on by the other Soldiers. Ivor, with his headphones on, is oblivious of what's happening. He throws a switch

Benji's Voice   "I had rather have
                                  Such men my friends than enemies. Go on,
                                  And see where Brutus be alive or dead;
                                  And bring us word unto Octavius' tent,
                                  How every thing is chanced."

Veronica Quick, that's our cue! Come on, Ed!

Ivor presses another switch. A fanfare sounds

The Soldiers, still with blue banners and shouting "A-Brutus! A-Brutus!", wave their swords and rush off DL

Dan now has his back to this exit and, with a sudden surge of energy, Ed attacks, driving Dan backwards to join the end of the line of Soldiers and disappear off stage

The Revd Elkins and Joan come in through the UL entrance

Joan Oh, look, Mr Millington's asleep.

Revd Elkins Huh! And I wonder where on earth Keith Horrobin's got to.

Apparently looking for Keith, he crosses to open the hatch into the Sydney Pratt Memorial Room. The minute the hatch is opened, there is a burst of girlish shouting and two cream trifles are slammed into the Revd's face. He staggers back, shutting the hatch doors. The shouting is silenced. The Revd Elkins turns to face the audience, feeling around with his hands. He inadvertently gropes Joan's bottom

Joan Ooh, vicar!
Revd Elkins (*feeling his way off* UR) I'm all dirty and disgusting.
Joan You certainly are.
Revd Elkins (*moving to the exit* UR) I must clean myself up.
Joan I quite agree.

The Revd Elkins exits UR

Joan, still a little trembly and, it has to be said, rather excited—after her grope, crosses to the table and sits in her secretarial chair. She picks up a shorthand pad and pencil, then looks at the sleeping Bernard and puts them down again

At this moment, from the UL *entrance, all the Soldiers—with Veronica entering first—come in backwards, waving their swords and shouting a confused mixture of "A-Brutus! A-Brutus!", "Gods for Antony and Octavius!" and various things in between*

Veronica slips and all the other Soldiers fall in a heap on top of her

The penultimate person to come in is Dan, now fighting for dear life and losing to the furiously energetic Ed

One of Ed's blows sends Dan's sword flying. As Dan turns to flee, Ed catches him a wallop on the bottom with the side of his sword and Dan, sobbing, collapses on top of the pile of Soldiers

Mr Quigley (*coming out of the shadows*) Yeah, attaboy! Well done, Ed!

Martyn comes furiously in from DL

Martyn What the hell do you think you're all doing! Brutus is meant to *lose*! You've ruined the play! *The wrong side won!*

Paula comes forward to take Ed's hand

Paula I wouldn't say that.

The Soldiers are picking themselves up off the floor

Martyn (*to the Soldiers*) Come on, all of you! Back on stage at once! We must do the whole of that scene again! This is the worst production I've ever been involved in!
Veronica (*the worm finally turning*) Well, whose fault do you think that is, Martyn?
Martyn (*wounded*) Shut up, Veronica! A director is only as good as the material he works with, and I'm working with utter rubbish! (*He leads off* DL) Come on, all of you! This whole show's a complete shambles!

He leads the Soldiers off stage

Dan remains lying on the floor, sobbing. Ed stays with Paula and turns to Mr Quigley

Ed Grandad, if Paula's mum finds us together, we'll be in dead schtuck. Isn't there anywhere we can go to be alone together—just for a little while?
Mr Quigley Yes, Ed. There certainly is. (*He crosses to his cubby-hole and bangs on the door*) All right, your time's up! Out you come! (*He uses his key to unlock the door*) Come on, out with you!

A very sheepish and somewhat ruffled Keith and Lydia emerge from the cubby-hole. Keith moves down stage. Lydia crosses to Bernard to check that he's all right

Mr Quigley gestures inside and Ed and Paula gleefully enter. Mr Quigley gives Ed the key and winks at him

You have a nice time now.
Ed Thank you, Grandad.

Ed and Paula disappear inside

Mr Quigley closes the door and it is heard to be locked from the inside

Keith is punching in a number on his portable phone

At that moment, Georgina comes stomping in from UR

Georgina Mr Quigley, have you seen my daughter?
Mr Quigley No, Mrs Hewlett.
Georgina Or that grandson of yours?
Mr Quigley (*shaking his head firmly*) Certainly not, Mrs Hewlett.
Georgina Well, I… (*Suddenly she is aware of Dan, lying on the floor and sobbing. She goes across to him*) Daniel… What on earth happened to you?
Dan (*crying like a baby*) I got hit on the bottom!

Georgina helps him up

Georgina (*helping him up*) Oh, you poor boy. Tell me about it.
Dan (*still crying*) I got into this fight. I didn't want to fight.

Georgina leads him gently UR

He was much bigger than me. And then… (*Wailing*) I got hit on the bottom!

Georgina and Dan exit UR

Keith (*switching off his portable phone*) Damn! I can't get through.
Mr Quigley What you trying to do then?
Keith I was trying to change some arrangements and I can't.
Mr Quigley (*very cheerfully*) Oh, bad luck.
Keith (*advancing on Mr Quigley*) Listen, this is all your fault, Mr Quigley. I'm going to see to it——

Lydia wakes Bernard. He suddenly rises to his feet, magnificent in his drunkenness, and turns on Keith

Bernard You are the man who has been to bed with my wife. (*He sways unsteadily*)

Mr Quigley moves across to near Ivor's table for a good view of the proceedings. He taps Ivor on the shoulder. Ivor takes off his headphones and they both watch the action with mounting enthusiasm

You are a bounder and a cad. You call me here on committee business...
Joan Is this committee business?
Bernard I beg your pardon?
Joan I mean—should I be taking minutes?
Bernard Take minutes if you like. (*He picks up a chair*) I will not take many minutes. (*He advances on Keith*) My revenge will be a matter of seconds.
Keith Look, what the hell're you playing at, Bernard?
Bernard I'm not playing. I am taking my revenge on the man who has had the nerve to go to bed with my wife—a wife whom, incidentally, I love very deeply...

Lydia reacts with surprise to this

...though perhaps I don't tell her that as often as I should. However, I hope that *this* will make up for all the times I haven't expressed myself before.
Keith What's "this"?
Bernard *This* is this.

Suddenly he raises the chair and brings it down hard on Keith's head. The seat of the chair flies out and Keith crumples to the floor. He is left sitting with the chair frame around his head

Keith Bernard...
Bernard (*raising a finger to silence him*) Don't speak. Oh, well, yes, it's all right, you can speak.
Keith What do you mean?
Bernard I mean it's all right, because you... (*he starts chuckling about what he's going to say*) ...because you'll be speaking "through the chair". (*He finds this inordinately funny and laughs outrageously. Then he recovers himself and speaks again*) Oh, I did enjoy that. (*He picks up another chair*) In fact, I enjoyed it so much I want to do it all over again! (*He advances on Keith*)

Keith picks himself up, removes the broken chair from around his neck and starts backing away

Keith Keep away from me, Bernard!

Bernard chases him around the table

Keith escapes into the Sydney Pratt Memorial Room

There is a burst of sounds of girlish mayhem while the door is open. It stops as soon as the door is closed. Bernard is about to follow Keith into the room

Lydia Don't bother, Bernard. You've beaten him! You've won! (*She throws her arms round him*) Oh, you were magnificent back then ... my ... my stallion!
Joan Should I be minuting this?
Bernard No, of course you shouldn't be minuting it, you stupid woman!
Joan Oh. (*She breaks down in tears*) Mr Millington...

She goes off UR, *wailing*

Bernard and Lydia ignore her and continue with their conversation

Lydia I didn't know you loved me, Bernard. I thought perhaps you'd stopped loving me.
Bernard Why should I have?
Lydia Well, because you're always so busy about everything, always so obsessed with your coloured stickers...
Bernard It's possible to be obsessed with coloured stickers and still love your wife, you know. (*He sways a little unsteadily and puts his hand to his head*) I think perhaps I'd better go home. I feel a little shaky. (*He crosses to get his coat*)
Lydia Yes, let's both go home, Bernard. Let's go straight home. And when we get home ... (*She puts her arms round him and purrs lasciviously*) let's go straight to bed, eh?
Bernard One moment. (*He reaches into his inside pocket for his filofax and opens it*) Ah, sorry, no can do. (*He points to something on the page*) Sex is blue. Look—no blue sticker. Sorry. (*He moves carefully down stage*) See you at home, love.

He goes out DC

Lydia (*with a little whimper of frustration*) Oh, Bernard. (*She thinks for a moment*) Bernard. (*She runs after him, almost pleading now*) Bernard! Bernard!

She follows her husband off

Ivor All going according to plan, Dad?
Mr Quigley Better than to plan, Ivor. And I think it's about to get even better still.

There is a shriek of homicidal girlish glee, as the hatch doors burst open

Keith, his suit covered with jelly and cream, is hoisted up by the little girls and thrust out of the hatch

He lands on the trolley, which is pushed out to go spinning across the room

The little girls, giggling with delight, come bouncing out of the hatch and the doors of the Sydney Pratt Memorial Room. They still look immaculate in their party frocks, though the expressions on their faces are pure evil. Candida is carrying three whipped cream aerosol cans

Davina follows the girls out with considerable dignity

She crosses to Keith's trolley and spins it round, so that he is facing her

Davina I thought you would like to know—officially, Keith—that our marriage is over.
Keith Don't be stupid, Davina. You can't just walk out!
Davina Watch me.
Keith But what're you going to do?
Davina (*after a moment's thought and a look at Ivor*) I'm going to move in with Ivor.

Ivor is as surprised as anyone to hear this. But certainly not displeased

Keith With Ivor? Ivor Quigley?
Davina Yes.
Keith But, for heaven's sake, Davina, why?

Davina Because he loves me, and I love him.

Keith But, Davina, you can't marry someone like that. He's common.

Davina (*furiously*) Common! Keith, Ivor doesn't even understand the meaning of the word "common". People who're secure in their class don't need to consider whether anyone's common or not. It's only people like you—the social climbers, the uneasy aspirers, the greedy upstarts—you're the ones for whom the word "common" was invented.

Keith (*picking himself up off the top of the trolley*) Davina, I'm not going to listen to any more of this. You're going to stay with me. A divorce at this stage in my career would be very damaging to me.

Davina Good.

Kylie and Anneka enter DC. They are tiny (ideally twins) and are both dressed in judo kit

Ivor Ah, hallo loves. Davina, these are my two little ones. Kylie and Anneka. Say hallo to Davina, loves.

Kylie (*sternly*) No. First we'll do what we came here to do.

Anneka (*indicating Keith; equally sternly*) Is he the one you meant, Grandad?

Mr Quigley (*chuckling*) Yes, yes. He's the one.

Keith backs away up stage as Kylie and Anneka advance on him. Then he tries to do a dash down stage between them. As he passes, they each grab an arm and throw him so that he rolls over and ends up crumpled against the back wall beneath the lifebelt. Kylie and Anneka turn gravely towards each other and bow. Candida moves forward to stand over Keith with a whipped cream aerosol

Keith Candida, you wouldn't.

Candida Wouldn't I just?

Keith But you love your Daddy really, don't you?

Candida No. I hate you, really. (*She turns to Kylie and Anneka, offering them whipped cream aerosol cans*) You two like to have a go?

Kylie
Anneka } (*running forward enthusiastically; together*) Ooh *yes*!

Mr Quigley flicks a switch on the console. A fanfare sounds, as Candida squirts whipped cream on to Keith's head. Kylie and Anneka do the same

*over other bits of him. They all continue until their aerosol cans are empty,
then stand back and look at their handiwork*

Candida You know, I think we three are going to get on really well.
Kylie ⎱ (*together*) You *bet*!
Anneka ⎰

Lord Grevesham enters DC

Lord Grevesham Good-evening. I'm looking for Keith Horrobin.
Mr Quigley (*coming forward and gesturing towards Keith*) Of course.
  Lord Grevesham, may I introduce you to our next parliamentary
  candidate...?

*The lifebelt on the wall above Keith falls down to hit him on the head. He
falls sideways*

Black-out

  *At the end of the curtain calls, all the cast go off stage, except for Mr
  Quigley. He picks up a large broom and, whistling tunelessly to himself,
  sweeps the floor of his Village Hall, as the audience leave*

FURNITURE AND PROPERTY LIST

Further dressing may be added at the director's discretion

ACT I

SCENE 1

On stage: Coats on hooks
"Sydney Pratt Memorial Room" sign
Grubby lifebelt encircling a shield
Old-fashioned wall-mounted calendar ("Monday 7th")
Green baize-covered table. *On it:* water carafes, agendas, note-pads,
    pencils, filofax
7 chairs
Electrical socket

Off stage: Keys (**Mr Quigley**)

Personal: **Keith:** personal organiser, portable phone
Bernard: wrist-watch
Mr Quigley: battered blue engagements diary, wrist-watch

SCENE 2

Re-set: Old-fashioned wall-mounted calendar ("Tuesday 8th")

Set: Ladder
Light bulb

Strike: Green baize-covered table. *On it:* water carafes, agendas, note-pads,
    pencils, filofax, portable phone
7 chairs

Off stage: Cassette player (**Tina**)
Exercise steps (**Henrietta et al**)
Sports bag (**Tina**)
Sports bag (**Georgina**)
Sports bag. *In it:* towels, leotard, shampoo, letter, etc. (**Paula**)

Personal:	**Ivor:** tool-belt with screwdrivers, hammers, small torch and other tools
	Lord Grevesham: wrist-watch, diary, pen
	Keith: wrist-watch
	Davina: handkerchief

SCENE 3

Re-set:	Old-fashioned wall-mounted calendar ("Wednesday 9th")
Set:	Chairs
	Magazine
	Coats on hooks
	Cardboard box. *In it:* copies of the play programme
Strike:	Ladder
	Cassette player
	Exercise steps
Personal:	**Rod:** copy of the play
	Martyn: ring-file
	Benji: crossword, pen, wrist-watch
	Veronica: copy of the play
	Ivor: copy of the play, **Paula**'s letter
	Mr Quigley: wrist-watch, coat, keys

SCENE 4

Re-set:	Old-fashioned wall-mounted calendar ("Thursday 10th")
Set:	Young people's anoraks
	Baseball jackets
	School bags. *In one of them:* bottle of vodka
	Table. *On it:* soft drink bottles and plastic beakers
Strike:	Chairs
	Magazine
	Coats on hooks
	Cardboard box. *In it:* copies of the play programme
Personal:	**Revd Elkins:** guitar
	Mr Quigley: blue Village Hall bookings book, ball-point pen

Keith: portable phone
Lord Grevesham: wrist-watch

ACT II

Re-set: Old-fashioned wall-mounted calendar ("Saturday 19th")

Set: Green baize-covered table. *On it:* water carafes, note-pads, pencils
             7 chairs
             Quasi-Roman banners and pikestaffs, with red decorations
             Quasi-Roman banners and pikestaffs, with blue decorations (one
                 broken)
             Small table. *On it:* console, tape recorder, speakers, headphones,
                 tapes, script, etc.
             Chair
             Balloons in the Sydney Pratt Memorial Room

Strike: Young people's anoraks
             Baseball jackets
             School bags. *In one of them:* bottle of vodka
             Table. *On it:* soft drink bottles and plastic beakers

Off stage: Serving trolley. *On it:* trays, silver-foil-wrapped packages, tray of
                 individual jellies, aerosol (**Davina**)
             Shopping bag (**Davina**)
             Pile of trays. *On them:* individual custard pies (**Candida**)
             Gift-wrapped present (**Chloe**)
             Gift-wrapped present (**Jessica**)
             Gift-wrapped present (**Antonia**)
             Gift-wrapped present (**Beatrice**)
             Gift-wrapped present (**Araminta**)
             Gift-wrapped present (**Perpetua**)
             Bag. *In it:* bottle of vodka (**Dan**)
             Sports bag (**Paula**)
             Sports bag (**Georgina**)
             Unicycle, big bulging bag. *In it:* mirror, tall hat with a dangly flower
                 on top, hooter with a bulb, playing cards, silk scarves, coloured
                 balls, gold rings, juggling clubs, etc. (**Professor Phun**)
             Professor Phun's trousers (**Davina**)
             3 whipped cream aerosol cans (**Candida**)

Personal: **Ed:** short, painted, wooden sword
             Martyn: ring-file, wrist-watch

Veronica: helmet
Mr Quigley: blue Village Hall bookings book, key
Davina: wrist-watch
Keith: portable phone, wrist-watch
Professor Phun: shapeless tweed hat, dead dove
Soldiers: swords and other weapons
Bernard: filofax

LIGHTING PLOT

Practical fittings required: hanging lamps with wide metal shades
Interior. The same throughout

ACT I, Scene 1

To open: Fade out house lights

Cue 1	**Bernard**: "…and it would therefore be my proposal…" *Fade up practical and general lighting; harsh light in the Sydney Pratt Memorial Room*	(Page 3)
Cue 2	**Bernard**: "In what way 'going funny'?" *Black-out*	(Page 11)
Cue 3	**Mr Quigley** opens the door of his cubby-hole *Cubby-hole lights spill out*	(Page 11)
Cue 4	**Mr Quigley** closes the door *Black-out*	(Page 11)
Cue 5	**Bernard**: "Yes, Joan, of course it's all right." *Snap on practical and general lighting*	(Page 11)
Cue 6	**Mr Quigley** disappears back inside the cubby-hole *Diminish lighting*	(Page 14)
Cue 7	The cubby-hole door closes *Black-out*	(Page 15)

ACT I, Scene 2

To open: Black-out

Cue 8	**Mr Quigley** is looking up at the hanging lights *Snap on hanging lights*	(Page 15)

Cue 9   **Mr Quigley**: "Yes, they're working."   (Page 15)
          Snap off hanging lights

Cue 10 **Mr Quigley**: "No, they're not."   (Page 15)
          Snap on hanging lights

Cue 11 **Mr Quigley**: "Yes, they are."   (Page 15)
          Snap off hanging lights

Cue 12 **Mr Quigley**: "No, they're not."   (Page 15)
          Snap on hanging lights except the DC *one*

Cue 13 **Davina** reaches into her pocket for a handkerchief   (Page 23)
          Snap on the DC *hanging light*

Cue 14 Once the aerobic class is established   (Page 28)
          Slowly fade to black-out

ACT I, SCENE 3

To open: Overall general lighting

Cue 15 **Lydia** shuts the cubby-hole door   (Page 42)
          Black-out

ACT I, SCENE 4

To open: Slowly bring up general lighting to reveal the scene; harsh lighting in
          the Sydney Pratt Memorial Room

Cue 16 **Mr Quigley** slams the Sydney Pratt door shut   (Page 60)
          Black-out

ACT II

To open: Overall general lighting; subtle lighting in the Sydney Pratt Memorial
          Room

Cue 17 **Keith** falls sideways   (Page 101)
          Black-out

EFFECTS PLOT

ACT I

Cue 1 **Revd Elkins**: "Oh. But surely——" (Page 7)
Portable phone ring

Cue 2 **Lydia** moves to the door to **Mr Quigley**'s cubby-hole (Page 8)
Portable phone ring

Cue 3 **Tina**: "With shoulder gyrations too!" (Page 26)
Music

Cue 4 Once the aerobic class is established (Page 28)
Slowly fade out music

Cue 5 **Ed** goes into the cubby-hole (Page 36)
Television football commentary while the door is open

Cue 6 **Keith** makes for **Mr Quigley**'s cubby-hole (Page 54)
Portable phone ring

Cue 7 **Mr Quigley** opens the cubby-hole door (Page 55)
Sound of television programme while the door is open

ACT II

Cue 8 **Ivor** turns a switch on the console (Page 62)
Lydia *and* **Rod's Voices** *as script page 62*

Cue 9 **Ivor** turns a switch on the console (Page 65)
Benji *and* **Martyn's Voices** *as script page 65*

Cue 10 **Ivor** turns a switch on the console (Page 67)
Mr Quigley's Voice *as script page 67*

Cue 11 **Ivor** turns a switch on the console   (Page 68)
          Rod's Voice *as script page 68*

Cue 12 **Ivor** unplugs his headphones   (Page 78)
          Rod's Voice *as script page 78*

Cue 13 **Ivor** turns a switch on the console   (Page 86)
          Benji *and* **Martyn's Voices** *as script page 86*

Cue 14 **Ivor** turns a switch on the console   (Page 87)
          Keith *and* **Lydia's Voices** *(including a kiss)*
              as script page 88

Cue 15 **Ivor** turns a switch on the console   (Page 89)
          Fanfare

Cue 16 **Ivor** turns a switch on the console   (Page 93)
          Benji's Voice *as script page 93*

Cue 17 **Ivor** turns a switch on the console   (Page 93)
          Fanfare

Cue 18 **Mr Quigley** turns a switch on the console   (Page 100)
          Fanfare

MADE AND PRINTED IN GREAT BRITAIN BY
LATIMER TREND & COMPANY LTD PLYMOUTH
MADE IN ENGLAND

Lightning Source UK Ltd.
Milton Keynes UK
UKHW022012211020
371989UK00006B/331